ANTARCTICA

ANTARCTICA

A HISTORY IN 100 OBJECTS

CONWAY

LONDON · OXFORD · NEW YORK · NEW DELHI · SYDNEY

CONWAY
Bloomsbury Publishing Plc
50 Bedford Square, London, WC1B 3DP, UK
29 Earlsfort Terrace, Dublin 2, Ireland

BLOOMSBURY, CONWAY and the Conway logo are trademarks of Bloomsbury Publishing Plc

First published in Great Britain, 2022

Copyright © Jean de Pomereu and Daniella McCahey, 2022

Jean de Pomereu and Daniella McCahey have asserted their right under the Copyright,
Designs and Patents Act, 1988, to be identified as Authors of this work

For legal purposes the Acknowledgements on pp.218–221
constitute an extension of this copyright page

A catalogue record for this book is available from the British Library

Library of Congress Cataloguing-in-Publication data has been applied for

ISBN: 978-1-8448-6621-2; ePub: 978-1-8448-6622-9; ePDF: 978-1-8448-6623-6

2 4 6 8 10 9 7 5 3 1

Design by Lee-May Lim
Typeset in Museo Sans by Carrdesignstudio
Printed and bound in India by Replika Press Pvt. Ltd.

To find out more about our authors and books visit www.bloomsbury.com
and sign up for our newsletters

Cover photographs © front cover: bottom left to top © Lutz Fitsch, courtesy of the Alfred Wegener
Institute, © Anne Noble, © Jean de Pomereu, spine: © Royal Belgian Institute of Natural Sciences,
back cover: top to bottom © Museene i Akershus, © Vestfold Museums, © British Antarctic Survey
Archives Service © Canterbury Museum, © Scott Polar Research Institute

CONTENTS

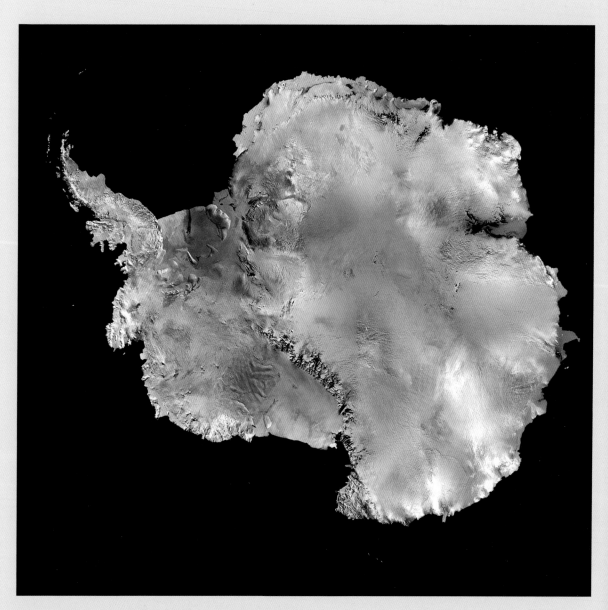

The continent of Antarctica. Satellite composite. © NASA, United States

INTRODUCTION

Mention the continent of Antarctica and the majority of people will imagine icy wastes – untouched, perhaps even unaffected, by human activities. Mention Antarctic life and they will think of the charismatic megafauna abounding in the region: whales breaching the water or slapping the surface with their tails, penguins frolicking on the ice, a leopard seal gliding threateningly past.

When it comes to historical studies, however, Antarctica often draws a blank. While a handful of stories of Antarctic heroism and tragedy are well known and oft repeated, how many books on world history mention or connect with the Antarctic? Moreover, despite representing nearly ten per cent of the Earth's total land mass, most world maps either distort the continent as a white strip at the bottom of the page or leave it out altogether. Even on terrestrial globes, Antarctica remains largely out of sight, concealed at the bottom of the Earth where the globemaker attaches the orb to its frame. The implication is that Antarctica is historically irrelevant and, aside from its scientific appeal, stands separate from economic, social, political and cultural concerns driving the rest of human history; a region about which historians could not possibly have anything useful to say.

In reality, Antarctic history is human history. Since the end of the 18th century, many global events have had direct reverberations on human engagements in the Antarctic, including imperialism and nationalism, the histories of various fields of science, gender and racial relations, and cultural imaginations of far-off spaces. Additionally, studies focusing on the Earth System have shown that Antarctica is deeply interdependent and intertwined with all aspects of our planet. Much of what happens in Antarctic environments, whether natural or human-induced, echoes across the Earth through the effects of glacial melt, the formation of the ozone hole, variations in the thermohaline circulation and the loss of biodiversity – to name a few of the most significant.

Many of the ideas behind this book were developed over the course of 2019–20, when the authors were selected to curate an exhibition on the history of Antarctica for the Mystic Seaport Museum in Connecticut, United States, in recognition of the bicentennial of the documented discovery of Antarctica. This was intended to be something different from other museum exhibitions on Antarctic history, the majority of which focus on exploration, science and environments within the context of specific periods and national perspectives. Instead, it would cover pre-discovery ideas of Antarctica, moving to the present day, touching on as many national Antarctic histories as possible. Once this exhibit was cancelled as a consequence of the COVID-19 pandemic in 2020, the authors decided to pursue their goal of telling a global history of Antarctica through material objects, but this time in the form of a book.

Using objects as a means to delve into wider histories is particularly apt when talking about the history of Antarctica. As with other extreme environments, living in the Antarctic is entirely dependent on the importation and use of technological solutions; its exploration is both enabled and constrained by the limits of available tools. Visiting Antarctica, the only continent with no agriculture or manufacturing, requires the judicious selection of objects and supplies that will help support both one's survival and more specific goals.

Objects also speak to heritage and its increasing importance on a continent that has no Indigenous population. Once they have been used in Antarctica, objects often take on emotional and material value. In some circumstances, they are formally protected, whether in museums or in Antarctica itself. Indeed, just as certain Antarctic areas are protected because of their environmental significance, since 1972, the Antarctic Treaty System has designated nearly a hundred 'Historic Sites and Monuments' under protection across the region. Much like these sites and monuments, the significance of historical objects is dependent on national perspectives on Antarctic heritage. Some countries that are especially proud of their Antarctic history and recognise its geopolitical relevance, even have dedicated organisations for protecting their national Antarctic heritage, whether on the continent or at home.

For this book, we have selected 100 objects to portray a history of Antarctica. This selection is not an attempt to tell the definitive history; it is simply one version from two historians with their own, often complementary, expertise and interests. We selected 100 objects from collections around the world because of the universality of that number, but we could have easily chosen to write a book containing 10, 50 or 500 objects. Unbound by nationality, history or physical constraints, ours is a global, multidisciplinary and nontemporal collection that seeks to reflect Antarctica's rich and varied

history in a holistic rather than a comprehensive manner.

We selected objects that speak to many themes in the history of Antarctica. Some highlight the various motivations that have driven people to visit the region. These include geographic and scientific curiosity, but also international collaboration, economic gain and personal or national glory. Indeed, some objects speak very specifically to Antarctica as a stage for the expression of nationalism and patriotism, personal fortitude, the importance of precedence, the ideation of masculinity or the exploitation of living resources.

As a continent officially designated for 'peace and science', according to the terms used in the 1959 Antarctic Treaty, it may be no surprise that we include several objects necessary for Antarctic knowledge-making. These range from the instrumentation brought onto the continent to specimens collected there and brought home. Likewise, many objects exemplify the spirit of friendship and community building imagined by the Antarctic Treaty System.

As this shows, human engagement with the Antarctic has not always had such positive connotations. If some people must be members of the Antarctic community, it requires that others be sidelined or excluded. A number of our chosen objects demonstrate the paradox of an Antarctica that must have some measure of exclusivity to maintain its projected exceptionality. Furthermore, while mostly imagined today as a fragile space, for many years the Antarctic was imagined more in terms of its hostility and alienness. As such, it was often the site of disaster, death, loss and longing.

Even prior to the discovery of the Antarctic continent in 1820, the exploitation of the Southern Ocean created a major economy fuelled by those who ventured south to fish and hunt in some of the world's roughest waters. More recently, with the birth of Antarctic tourism in the mid-20th century, it was the contemplation of mighty glaciers and charismatic megafauna that resulted in the development of a new economy, one that brings more people to Antarctica than any other human activity. Our increasing human footprint both in the region and the global environment more broadly has in turn led to an Antarctica tainted by pollution. Indeed, we would be remiss to discuss Antarctic history without addressing objects that speak to its multifaceted role in the global economy.

Even when its history disappoints, however, Antarctica continues to spark human curiosity, creativity, contemplation and wonder. Once and always a site for the imagination, the southern continent channels our thoughts and interrogations to the otherworldly. With this in mind, we invite you to begin a journey through Antarctic space and time as you use the objects in this book to peer into the minds of Antarctic travellers past and present. As you start this journey, perhaps you will consider what objects you think would best represent your own encounters with the Antarctic, be they physical or in your imagination.

Antarctic Shrine, by Standish Backus, 1957. © Courtesy of the United States Navy History and Heritage Command, Washington DC, United States

01

WORLD MAP

Millennia before it was first discovered, the idea of Antarctica resulted in a whole variety of imaginary projections and interpretations. Its imaginary mapping can be traced as far back as the 5th century BC, when the Greek philosopher Parmenides divided the world into five parallel zones, believing that a southern land mass must exist to counterbalance the known lands of the north. This idea was retained by Aristotle in his *Meteorology* of *c*.330 BC.

Four centuries later, a more influential mappa mundi was proposed by Ptolemy in his *Geographia*, in which he joined the southern regions of Africa with an imaginary southern land mass stretching right across the bottom of the map and slightly further north than the Tropic of Capricorn. It was described as terra incognita.

With the Renaissance and the emergence of maritime exploration, maps became essential instruments for scholasticism, geographic expansion and trade. A new cartographic tool was introduced during this period – the globe – and in 1531, the French cartographer and mathematician Oronce Fine produced a groundbreaking bi-cordiform world map, in which he represented Antarctica as a massive, solid and largely empty landmass extending across the lower latitudes and the South Pole.

Fine's map inspired France's Dieppe school of cartography, the Brabantian cartographer Abraham Ortelius and the Flemish cartographer and engraver Gerardus Mercator, who in his mappa mundi of 1569 also represented a vast and solid *Terra Australis*, engulfing what we now know as Australia. Although some 17th-century cartographers produced world maps where the southern continent was altogether absent (thus illustrating the true state of knowledge at the time), it was Mercator's projection that remained dominant well into the 18th century.

Among those who perpetuated Mercator's projection was the Jesuit missionary Matteo Ricci, who produced the first Chinese world maps with collaborators such as the engraver Li Zhizao. The oldest is the 1584 *Yudi Shanhai Quantu*, followed in 1602 by the woodblock-printed *Kunyu*

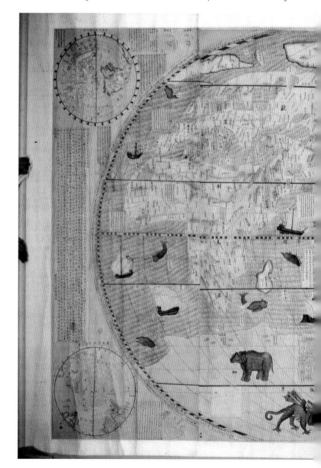

Wanguo Quantu, commissioned by the Wanli Emperor. Hugely significant in its combination of European and Chinese geographic knowledge at the time, the *Kunyu Wanguo Quantu* places China near the centre of the world and features Mercator's *Terra Australis* with the inscription: 'Few have reached these southern regions. So the things are not explored yet.' Slightly later, hand-drawn manuscript versions such as this one populate *Terra Australis* with both real and imaginary creatures – elephants, crocodiles, rhinoceros, lions, ostriches and dragons, as well as sea creatures and ships along its coastline.

Indeed, similarly imaginative visions of *Terra Australis* by Western cartographers inspired Scottish hydrographer Alexander Dalrymple to advocate in 1769 the exploration of the South Seas to find the hidden southern continent, which he believed was of 'greater extent than the whole civilised part of Asia, from Turkey to the eastern extremity of China', with a population of more than 50 million. Seeking this hidden southern continent was a major motivation for the exploratory voyages of James Cook.

Kunyu Wanguo Quantu (Map of the Myriad Countries of the World), 1608. © Getty Images/Nanjing Museum

02

TAOKA

Although there was no evidence of European incursions into Antarctic waters until the 17th century, there are traditions of polar explorations from other parts of the world.

The most notable of these explorers is likely the 7th-century Polynesian navigator Ui-te-Rangiora. According to Maori oral tradition, Ui-te-Rangiora led a fleet, headed by his own great canoe, *Te Ivi-o-Atea*, and sailed south from Rarotonga in the Cook Islands until he encountered 'rocks that grow out of the sea', or the icebergs and ice floes of the Southern Ocean. While there is no documentary evidence of Ui-te-Rangiora's travels, archaeologists have shown the presence of Polynesian explorers and even settlers in the subantarctic as early as the 13th century.

In 1989, the Southland Art Museum and the New Zealand Department of Conservation facilitated a visit to the subantarctic Auckland Islands, north of the Antarctic Convergence. On this visit, potter Chester Nealie discovered an example of a hei matau (fish hook) on Enderby Island. This taoka, or 'treasured possession', later dated to the 14th century, is made from marine ivory and comprises notches for bait and a line. In 1998, an expedition to Enderby Island led by New Zealand archeologist Atholl Anderson found ovens, tools and midden heaps of mussel shells and bird and seal bones. This expedition showed that at least 500 years before its European 'discovery' in 1806, this island had not only been explored by Polynesian navigators, but that a settlement of Polynesians and their dogs had colonised it, living there for at least one summer.

It serves as a reminder that polar exploration was not only a European interest. On the contrary, journeys south predated those by the white men traditionally considered to be the pioneering explorers of the Antarctic. As symbolised by a sculpture, installed outside New Zealand's Scott Base in 2013, by the Maori artist Fayne Robinson, engagements with Indigenous knowledge are a growing component of scientific and conservation efforts in these regions.

Hei matau (fish hook), 14th century. Enderby Island. Marine ivory, modified with stone tools.
© Southland Museum and Art Gallery, Niho o te Taniwha, Invercargill, New Zealand (ref. Z.4340)

03

CHRONOMETER

As he set sail in July 1772, James Cook's mission was to circumnavigate the globe and venture as far south as possible in search of a great land mass at the South Pole. To achieve these objectives, the British Admiralty provided Cook with two vessels, HMS *Resolution* and HMS *Adventure*, over 200 officers and men, and a marine chronometer to help calculate longitude.

An exact duplicate of acclaimed British instrument-maker John Harrison's H4 time-keeper, the K1 chronometer was created by watchmaker Larcum Kendall in 1769. Although it measured just 13cm (5in) in diameter, its complexity and the precision of its mechanism meant that it cost an expensive £450 to manufacture, or about a tenth of what it cost the Admiralty to purchase the *Resolution*.

Assigning this sum to a chronometer whose efficacy still needed testing was justified by its potential to help keep track of a ship's position over a long sea journey. At this time, the calculation of latitude was relatively straight-forward, consisting of measuring the angle of the sun at noon or the angle of Polaris from the horizon. Determining longitude, however, required the comparison of local time at a ship's given location with the known time at a place of reference, in this instance Greenwich. While this could be achieved through the observation of regular celestial motions, ship movement and instability made it extremely difficult and often imprecise.

K1 chronometer used on James Cook's second voyage, 1772–75. © National Maritime Museum, Greenwich, United Kingdom

Men harvesting ice in *The Ice Islands*, by William Hodges, in James Cook's *Voyage Towards the South Pole, and Round the World. Performed in His Majesty's ships the Resolution and Adventure, in the years, 1772, 1773, and 1775, 1777.*
© Courtesy of University of California, Irvine Special Collections & Archives, United States

The solution lay in designing and manufacturing a timekeeper whose accuracy would not be affected by the motion of ships, nor by corrosive salt air and variations in temperature, pressure or humidity as vessels sailed through different climatic zones. Producing such an item became one of the greatest engineering challenges of all time.

Initially sceptical about the K1, Cook soon recognised the chronometer's reliability and began to refer to it as his 'trusty friend the Watch' or his 'never-failing guide'. Although the K1 did not help Cook to locate a southern continent, it did allow him to chart his course with unparalleled precision, discovering and claiming vast territories on behalf of the British Empire and making the first three documented forays south of the Antarctic Circle in 1773 and 1774.

Accurate timepieces like this chronometer were of the utmost importance to Antarctic exploration. Until the introduction of GPS in the 1970s, explorers in Antarctica – where there is generally a lack of fixed land points, as well as little distinction between night and day – continued to use chronometers not only for determining the time, but also for determining their whereabouts and navigating their way to safety.

04

COMMEMORATIVE MEDAL

The question of who was first to sight the Antarctic mainland remains a source of heated debate. While some argue that it was Irish-born British Royal Navy officer Edward Bransfield's sighting of the Trinity Peninsula on 30 January 1820 and others believe it was the American seal hunter Nathaniel Palmer on 17 November 1820, the most widely circulated scenario is that it was Fabian Gottlieb von Bellingshausen on 27 January 1820.

A distinguished officer and cartographer in the Russian Imperial Navy, Bellingshausen had already participated in the first Russian circumnavigation of the globe in 1803–06 when he was chosen to lead the first Russian Antarctic expedition and instructed by Alexander I to push as far south as possible in search of a southern continent. Bellingshausen was provided with two cumbersome vessels, the *Vostok*, which he commanded, and the *Mirny*, commanded by Mikhail Lazarev, both of which are named on

this 1819 commemorative medal, also featuring a profile of the emperor.

Bellingshausen departed from the Russian port of Kronstadt on 4 June 1819 with supplies for two years that included 28 tons of corned beef and 3,926 litres (864 gallons) of vodka. His ships crossed the Antarctic Circle – the first time since James Cook – on 15 January 1820, and reached 69°25' South on 27 January, unable to proceed any further because of the density of the pack

Medal commemorating the voyage of the *Vostok* and *Mirny*, 1819–24.
© National Maritime Museum, Greenwich, United Kingdom

The *Vostok* and the *Mirny* among icebergs. *Aurora Australis* by Pavel Mikhailov, 1821–24. © State Historical Museum, Moscow, Russia

ice. From there, Bellingshausen later described having seen 'ice-covered mountains', 'icy hills' or 'continuous ice' (depending on the translation). He also introduced the term 'main ice' to describe what he had seen on reaching his second furthest south at 69°7' on 17–18 February 1820.

The use of language and reliability of interpretation, especially when translating, is indeed where complications begin in defining Bellingshausen's place in Antarctic history. While some historians point out that his descriptions may just as easily have been of tabular icebergs, others argue that the ice edge of Antarctica along Queen Maud Land is constantly changing and difficult to differentiate from other icy formations, especially in overcast conditions.

There are also questions as to why Bellingshausen only mentioned a 'continent of ice' in a report written months after the supposed sightings, and some argue that later interpretations and translations may have been historically biased. Add to this the ongoing debates about the possible extent of particular ice shelves in 1820 and the only certainty is that Bellingshausen later sighted Alexander I Land, then thought to be attached to the Antarctic Peninsula, as his circumpolar voyage was drawing to a close in 1821.

The difficult question of what Bellingshausen saw and when he saw it may never be settled, but it nevertheless remains key to Antarctic history. Moreover, as suggested by this commemorative medal, it remains central to Russia's national and exploratory history, with the name *Vostok* later adopted for the Soviet Union's most remote Antarctic station, as well as for the *Vostok* space programme, which brought the first man into orbit in 1961.

05

LOGBOOK

At the start of the 19th century, driven by the demand for fur clothing in the United States and Europe as well as the burgeoning trade between the United States and China, hunters widened their scope in the search for fur seals. Nathaniel B Palmer, a young sealing captain from Stonington, Connecticut, sailed his crew southwards in the austral summer of 1820 on board the sloop *Hero*, searching for seal rookeries in the Southern Ocean.

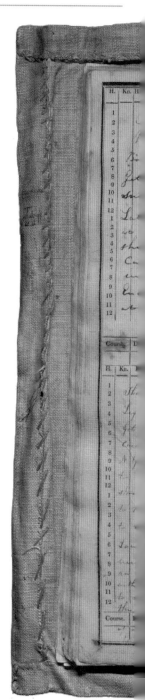

On 17 November 1820, Palmer sighted land, an event that he recorded in his logbook: 'At 4 A.M. made sail in shore and Discovered-a-strait-Tending SSW&NNE it was Literally filled with Ice and the shore inaccessible thought it not Prudent to Venture in we Bore away to the Northw'd and saw two small Islands and the shore every where Perpendicular we stood across toward Freseland [Livingston Island] course NNW the Latitude [sic] of the mouth of the straight was 63.45 S End with fine weather SSW.' This land sighting was later recognised as the tip of the Antarctic Peninsula.

Logbooks were updated daily, recording a ship's location and local weather as well as noting important events in the management, operation and navigation of a ship. Palmer's highlights the significance of logbooks as evidence for discovery. In fact, it remains uncertain as to whether Palmer was indeed the first to catch a glimpse of the Antarctic continent in 1820, or it was the Russian Imperial Navy officer Fabian von Bellingshausen or the Irish-born British Royal Navy officer Edward Bransfield. Today, historians continue to use logbooks to reconstruct polar journeys, attempting to settle these debates.

Although Palmer was likely not the first to sight the Antarctic continent, his legacy remains significant. First, his discovery of new rich sealing grounds spurred a rush of activity by sealers such as James Weddell, for whom the Weddell Sea and the Weddell seal are named. Palmer's connection to the region has also served as a way for the United States Antarctic Program (USAP) to link their current activities in the region to past incursions.

Not only is Palmer remembered through place names such as Palmer Land, the Palmer Archipelago, Hero Bay and Stonington Island along the Antarctic Peninsula, but the USAP operates an Antarctic research vessel named *Nathaniel B. Palmer* and maintains Palmer research station, first established in 1968 on Anvers Island, in the vicinity of past hunting grounds and now recovering fur seal colonies.

Logbook of Nathaniel Palmer's ship *Hero*. © Palmer-Loper Family Papers. Courtesy of the Manuscript Division, Library of Congress, Washington DC, United States

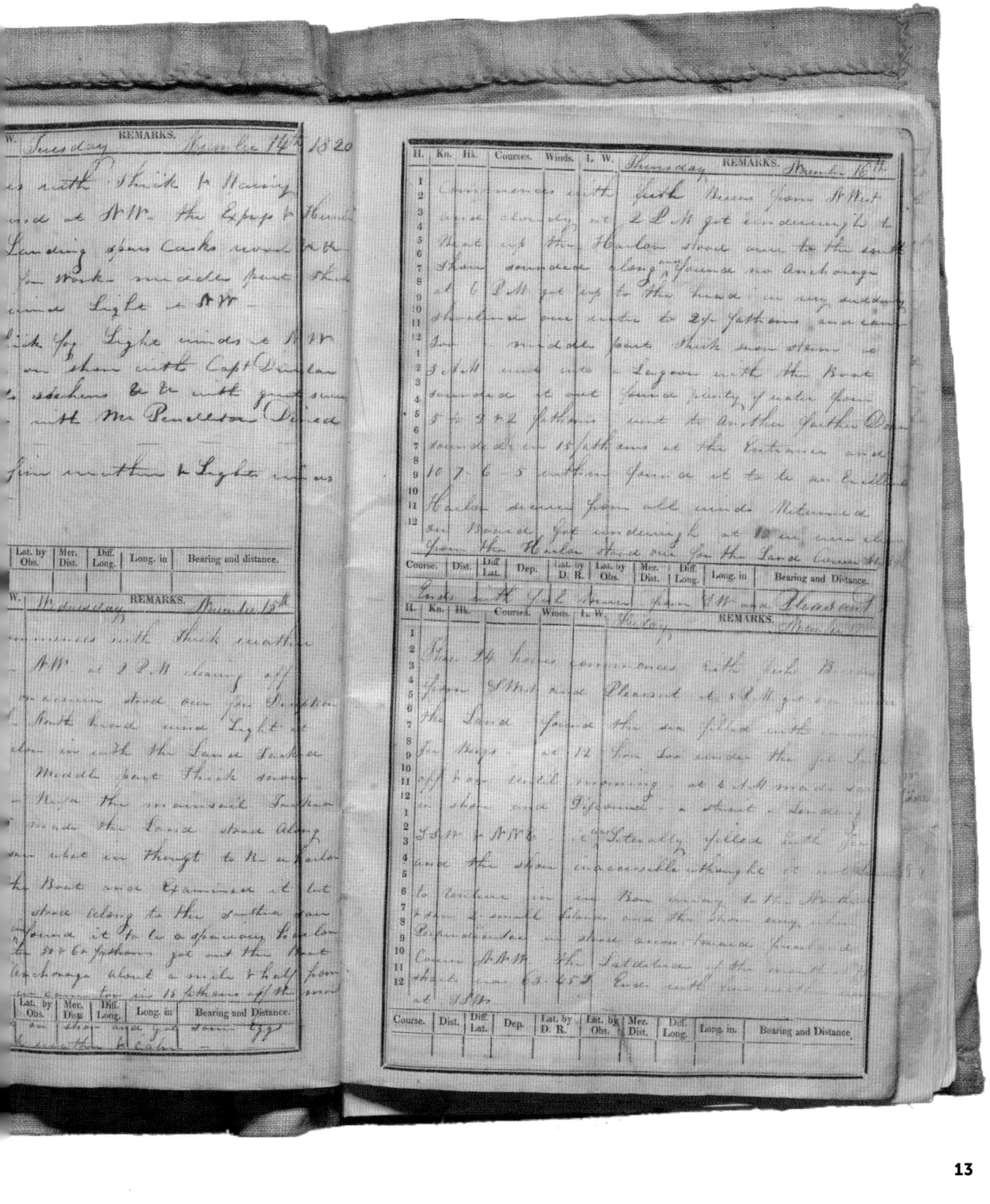

06

FUR SEAL COAT

Following their first sighting of the Antarctic Peninsular from their sealing vessel, *Hero*, on 17 November 1820, Connecticut ship captain Nathaniel Palmer and his crew quickly recognised the economic opportunity offered by the region's rich sealing grounds.

Their discovery was soon followed by a rush of other sealing ships and resulted in the slaughter of fur seals along the beaches of Antarctic islands. Fur sealing had a boom-and-bust quality; once a region was picked over, the sealers moved on to more fertile grounds. As early as 1829, British naturalist James Eights lamented the loss of the fur seal on the Antarctic Peninsula: 'This beautiful little animal was once most numerous here, but was almost exterminated by the sealers, at the time these islands were first discovered.'

By 1833, at least 7 million fur seals had been killed in the Antarctic and subantarctic. Even in the 19th century, hunters were concerned about the sustainability of these populations. In 1896, Norwegian whaler Henrik Bull recalled the history of early fur seal hunting grounds: 'scene[s] of a butchery even more insane and unworthy of civilised man'. Instead, he argued for 'substituting a system of regulated capture'.

In the 19th century, seal fur was used for clothing in many parts of the world and became an important component of European and American trade with China. British sealer and Antarctic explorer James Weddell even lamented the American strength in this area, where, carrying fur seal skins to China, 'they frequently obtained a price of $5–6 USD apiece. It is generally known that the English did not enjoy the same privilege; by which means the Americans took entirely off our hands this valuable article of trade.'

Another example of clothing made from Antarctic fauna. *Portrait of James Francis Smith* wearing a coat made from penguin skins, acquired on his father's whaling voyage to Desolation Island, on board the Chelsea. By Isaac Sheffield, 1837. © Lyman Allyn Art Museum, New London, Connecticut, United States

Woman's seal fur coat, 1880s. © College of Education/Human Ecology Historic Costume & Textiles Collection, The Ohio State University, Columbus, United States

The richness of Antarctic fur sealing grounds did not last long. By the second half of the 19th century, the population had been so decimated that hunters in search of fur seals moved on to the Arctic. But the damage was done and ships continued their incursions into Antarctic waters in search of other exploitable species.

07

WOOD BLOCK

The United States Exploring Expedition of 1838–42 was focused on exploring and surveying the Pacific Ocean. Led by US Navy Lieutenant Charles Wilkes, it included six ships and a large party of scientists. In January 1840, the expedition explored the eastern coastline of Antarctica. Although there had been many confirmed and reported sightings of Antarctic land since 1820, Wilkes made the weighty claim that it was his expedition that had for the first time sighted the actual continental landmass of Antarctica.

Wilkes frequently commented on both the beauty and the desolation of these regions. He was particularly impressed by the many large, tabular icebergs: 'These tabular bergs are like masses of beautiful alabaster: a verbal description of them can do little to convey the reality to the imagination of one who has not been among them. If an immense city of ruined alabaster palaces can be imagined, of every variety of shape and tint, and composed of huge piles of buildings grouped together, with long lanes or streets winding irregularly through them, some faint idea may be formed of the grandeur and beauty of the spectacle. The time and circumstances under which we were viewing them, threading our way through these vast bergs, we know not to what end, left an impression upon me of these icy and desolate regions that can never be forgotten.'

Wood block showing a tabular iceberg, used for printing Charles Wilkes' *Narrative of the U.S. Exploring Expedition*, 1844. © Division of Work and Industry, National Museum of American History, Smithsonian Institution, Washington DC, United States

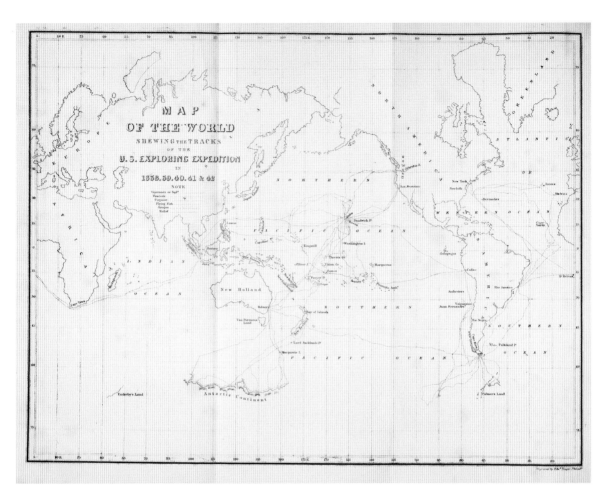

Map of the supposed Antarctic continent from Charles Wilkes' *Narrative of the U.S. Exploring Expedition*, 1845.
© Courtesy of the Linda Hall Library of Science, Engineering and Technology, Kansas City, United States

Wilkes drew the tabular iceberg on this wood block, which was engraved by American artist BF Childs and printed by Philadelphia printer C Sherman within Wilkes' *Narrative of the U.S. Exploring Expedition, During the Years 1838, 1839, 1840, 1841, 1842*.

The United States Exploring Expedition played a major role in the development of 19th-century science, but it was not an unqualified success. In 1841, the sloop-of-war USS *Peacock* went aground near the Columbia River and was lost.

Additionally, after an incident during which two party members were killed while bartering in Fiji, the Americans killed approximately 80 Fijians in reprisal. This was only one of several violent encounters with Indigenous peoples. Many of the specimens collected were lost or damaged before they could be catalogued. Finally, upon return, Wilkes was court-martialled and charged with the loss of the *Peacock,* regular mistreatment of his subordinate officers and excessive punishment of his sailors. He was acquitted on most charges.

08

BURIAL MONUMENT

At 5.45pm on 8 May 1842, a packed train carrying passengers back from Versailles to Paris after a day of celebrations and water displays in honour of King Louis Philippe catastrophically derailed and burst partly into flames. It was France's first major rail accident. Among those who perished was the famous navigator Jules Sébastien César Dumont d'Urville, his wife and their two sons.

Born in Normandy in 1790, d'Urville's many achievements include securing the acquisition of the classical Greek statue the *Venus de Milo* for France and recovering the remains of the 18th-century explorer Jean-François de Galaup, comte de La Pérouse from the South Pacific. Most important in the context of Antarctica was his leadership of the first maritime expedition to determine the approximate position of the South Magnetic Pole. He also discovered new coastal stretches of East Antarctica and identified a new species of penguin, both of which he named after his wife, Adélie. Thus the tragic irony that a man who had three times circumnavigated the Earth and explored some of its most hostile regions in a wooden sailing ship, *l'Astrolabe*, died in the spectacular failure of a metallic emblem of the Industrial age.

On board the same train that day was the young architect Simon-Claude Constant-Dufeux, who survived the crash and was commissioned to design the burial monument of d'Urville and his family in the Montparnasse cemetery in Paris. Unveiled

Burial monument designed by Simon-Claude Constant-Dufeux for Jules Sébastien César Dumont d'Urville and his family at the Montparnasse cemetery in Paris. By Léon Leymonnerye, 1871.
© Courtesy of the Musée Carnavalet, Paris, France

before a large crowd two and a half years after the accident, the monument triggered immediate surprise, criticism and mocking for its bizarre phallic appearance, as well as for its flamboyant polychromy (the paintwork with which it was decorated and which has now mostly disappeared). Some complained about its absence of Christian symbols, while others compared it to fetish objects displayed in shop windows in seedy Paris streets.

The strong reactions triggered by the grave largely ignored Constant-Dufeux's Romantic intentions in designing what is certainly the most thoughtful and innovative among the many memorials to explorers. Rather than simply representing d'Urville in a heroic or conquering stance, Constant-Dufeux took advantage of the freedoms offered by funerary art to express what he regarded as the utopian potential of both architecture and exploration: a potential that,

although impossible for him to predict at the time, now also seems to correspond to Antarctica as a continent for 'all mankind'. From a contemporary perspective, the phallic appearance of the burial memorial also seems to suggest the penetrative nature of exploring 'virgin' territories.

In fact, despite its appearance, Constant-Dufeux's monument to the d'Urville family is a unifying amalgamation of architectures as disparate in time and style as Neolithic monoliths, Gaulian menhirs, Egyptian obelisks and classical columns. It also pays reverence to science through the mathematical exactitude of its parabolic profile, while reviving Gothic and classical traditions through its polychromy. Finally, it reminds the public of d'Urville's achievements through the inscriptions and reliefs around the base of the monument, the largest among them being 'POLE SUD' accompanied by an etching of l'Astrolabe.

Entering the Pack Ice, by Louis Le Breton, in Jules Dumont d'Urville's *Voyage au Pôle Sud, 1842–54*. © Courtesy of the Linda Hall Library of Science, Engineering & Technology, Kansas City, United States

09

MAGNETIC DIP CIRCLE

In the mid-19th century, Britain's interest in the Antarctic was primarily driven by the Magnetic Crusade, a major data-collecting enterprise that established geomagnetic observatories in British imperial territories around the world, and comprised the quest for the magnetic poles. These investigations were crucial not only for the academic study of magnetism, but also as a practical aid for navigation.

In 1839, the Royal Navy and the Royal Society organised an expedition to journey to the Antarctic and locate the Magnetic South Pole. The expedition ships were HMS *Erebus* and HMS *Terror* (later famously lost in the Arctic during John Franklin's expedition). The commander was James Clark Ross, who had already taken part in the search for the magnetic North Pole.

Determining the location of the Magnetic South Pole was 'regarded as a first and, indeed indispensable step to the construction of a rigorous and complete theory of terrestrial magnetism'. To help achieve his mission, Ross took with him a magnetic dip circle such as the one shown here. The instrument was used to measure the angle between the horizon and the Earth's magnetic field (the dip angle). While dip circles had existed since the 16th century, the version Ross took on the expedition could be used at sea on board a moving vessel thanks to a later improvement by the British inventor Robert Were Fox.

Brass dip circle used on board the *Erebus* or *Terror* during the 1845 British Northwest Passage Expedition. © National Maritime Museum, Greenwich, United Kingdom

Mount Erebus and Mount Terror, on Ross Island in the Ross Sea, from Joseph Hooker, *The Botany of the Antarctic Voyage of HM Discovery Ships* Erebus *and* Terror, 1844. © Courtesy of the Linda Hall Library of Science, Engineering & Technology, Kansas City, United States

Ross' expedition departed England in August of 1839. In January 1841, he wrote: 'We now shaped our course directly for the Magnetic Pole ... Our hopes and expectations of attaining that interesting point were now raised to the highest pitch, too soon, however, to suffer as severe a disappointment ... the land interposed an insuperable obstacle to our direct approach ... we could not but feel disappointed in our expectation of shortly reaching the magnetic pole.' Despite this setback, the ships continued to seek the magnetic pole, until Ross finally lamented in February 1841: 'I felt myself compelled to abandon the perhaps too ambitious hope that I had so long cherished of being permitted to plant the flag of my country on both magnetic poles of our globe.'

Although the Ross expedition did not reach the Magnetic South Pole, it 'had approached the pole some hundreds of miles nearer than any

of our predecessors; and from the multitude of observations that were made in so many directions from it, its position may be determined with nearly as much accuracy as if we actually reached the spot itself'. From these observations, the scientists could infer the pole's position measurements taken from the sea, resulting in the first definitive charts of magnetic declination, magnetic dip and magnetic intensity.

These magnetic charts contributed to the Royal Navy's ability to navigate the oceans, and secured Britain's imperial prosperity and security.

10

SEALING CLUB

Through the 19th century, Antarctic waters teemed with ships seeking riches from the Southern Ocean. Besides the lucrative fur seal grounds, hunters also sought the oil-rich elephant seals and whales that lived in these waters. In this period, there was much overlap in the whaling and sealing communities. This work was hard and dangerous. The men's days were filled with monotonous, often back-breaking labour, punctuated by short periods of danger and excitement. Many men filled what little free time they had available pursuing artistic endeavours and creating items that could serve as keepsakes of their travels, or items that they could sell to the willing collector. Articles made from the body parts of seals, walruses and whales were often targets of this artistic expression.

Whale and seal bones, which were plentiful, could be shaped into tools, like knife handles, pipes and clubs. Scrimshaw engravings showed images of varying artistry and detail, depending on the skills of the artist.

This club, created by skilful shaping of a seal or walrus penis bone, was useful for hunters in search of seals. Fur seals were usually killed by a firm hit over the head with a club, to leave its skin undamaged. Elephant seals, in contrast, often

Sealing club made of the *baculum* (penis bone) of a seal or walrus. © Mystic Seaport Museum, Connecticut, United States (ref. 1939.1256)

Heard Island, South Indian Ocean. Artist unknown, 19th century. © Mystic Seaport Museum, Connecticut, United States (ref. 1933.26)

too large to kill in this manner, were lanced or shot before their bodies were stripped of their skin and broken down for blubber. This was a grisly business.

Seals were easy prey and it was not difficult for the hunters to drive them to the beaches, lance them through the heart, drain their blood and remove their blubber. One scientist, on board a whaling vessel in 1912, was dismayed by his 'blood-thirsty shipmates … aiming to murder them'. A later account tells of a hunt where '[on] the beach there were perhaps a dozen corpses, their heads from which blood oozed slowing over the stones towards the sea … to make death more certain,

each man, with his sharp triangular knife, made a deep red gash on the neck, thus severing the carotid artery, and the blood jetted out…' The oil derived from these actions was used for lamp fuel through the 19th century and as an industrial lubricant through the 20th centruy.

Beyond the commercial sealing industry, Antarctic scientists and explorers killed and ate seals, or fed them to their dogs. The Convention for the Conservation of Antarctic Seals was initiated in 1972, although, by that time, changing socio-cultural sentiments regarding seals and the availability of synthetic alternatives meant that few nations engaged in the practice.

FISH SPECIMEN

The day of deliverance finally came on 14 March 1899. Adrien de Gerlache's *Belgica* had been beset in sea ice of the Bellingshausen Sea for more than a year, unintentionally becoming the first expedition to winter in the Antarctic. For the past month, using ice saws and tonite to free up a channel through which to escape, the 17 surviving men had scrambled desperately to free their vessel before another winter descended upon them. After pushing against them, the wind finally turned in their favour.

Emil Racovitza, the expedition's Romanian biologist, expressed the crew's mixed feelings: 'I must admit that the sentiment derived from our liberation was not the one that our imagination had projected during our captivity. We were certain that having reached the ice edge, we would flee as quickly as possible the detestable and deserted sea ice. But it was not like that: we stayed one more day to trawl and make soundings, and when the moment came to head north, we were surprised to feel some regret about leaving the pack.'

On that day, among the specimens their trawl recovered from a depth of 2,800m (9,186ft) were two *Coryphaenoides lecointei*, a deep-sea cod-like fish (Gadiformes) that is part of the *Macrouridae* family. Measuring 42cm (16.5in) and 19cm (7.5in) in length, the specimens were one of the most notable catches of the *Belgica* expedition and the first belonging to that particular species. Preserved in alcohol, they found their way into the collections of the Royal Belgian Museum of Natural History, where they can still be seen today.

The *Belgica* was not the first expedition to carry out oceanographic work in the Southern Ocean. That honour goes to the *Challenger* expedition, which laid the foundations of oceanography during its circumnavigation of the globe in 1872–76 and penetrated the Antarctic Circle north of Queen Maud Land as it sailed eastwards in 1874. The scientists on board HMS *Challenger* used a variety of dredges and trawls to collect biological samples from the sea floor. They collected so many that it took several years to classify and publish the expedition's 50 beautifully illustrated volumes of scientific findings.

Crew of the *Belgica* sounding in the Southern Ocean, c.1897. By Frederick Cook. © Getty Images/Royal Geographical Society

Coryphaenoides lecointei fish specimen collected on 15 March 1899 during Adrien de Gerlache's Belgian Antarctic Expedition 1897–99. © Courtesy of the Royal Belgian Institute of Natural Sciences, Brussels

Today, the interest in Southern Ocean fish is driven at least as much by consumption as by research. This has resulted in increasingly stringent international regulation of Southern Ocean fisheries through the Convention for the Conservation of Antarctic Marine Living Resources (CCAMLR). Established in 1982, CCAMLR oversees the exploitation of species such as Patagonian and Antarctic toothfish, often referred to as 'white gold' because of their increasing popularity in restaurants worldwide, where they are often presented as 'Chilean sea bass'.

12

HUT

One of Antarctica's defining characteristics is the absence of Indigenous human populations. Indeed, it was only in 1899 that the first buildings came to be erected on the continent, the earliest predecessor to the 80 or so functioning research stations in Antarctica today.

The first two Antarctic huts were constructed as a wintering base by Anglo-Norwegian explorer Carsten Borchgrevink's *Southern Cross* expedition, 1898–1900. They are located in the middle of the world's largest Adélie penguin rookery at Cape Adare, where the Ross Sea connects with the wider Southern Ocean – one of the most inhospitable places on Earth.

Borchgrevink had previously landed at Cape Adare in 1895 as a member of a Norwegian whaling expedition led by Henrik Bull, the first undisputed landing on Antarctica's continental landmass. While ashore, Borchgrevink collected geological specimens and lichen, and after the ship's return to Melbourne, he began to plan his own scientific and geographic expedition, including a winter at Cape Adare. Despite conflicting interests with the Royal Geographical Society, which was planning its own expedition, Borchgrevink eventually secured the financial backing of the British magazine publisher George Newnes.

Borchgrevink's two huts, which he named Camp Ridley, were built from Baltic pine. The larger hut, measuring 36sq m (388sq ft), served as living and sleeping quarters for the ten-man shore party. It had a double floor, outer walls insulated with papier mâché, and the roof was later covered with seal skins weighed down by bags of coal and boulders. The smaller hut, measuring 30sq m (323sq ft), was fitted with a small photographic darkroom and used for the storage of scientific equipment, food supplies, a collection of guns and 500 Union Jacks, with which they planned to claim Antarctic regions for the British Empire. In addition to the men, the shore party included 75 Siberian dogs housed in kennels fashioned from packing cases.

The winter months proved difficult. Despite the hut's sliding panels and curtains designed to provide some privacy, tensions quickly arose. This was not helped by Borchgrevink's poor leadership skills, nor by the fierce winter storms that made the hut feel precarious despite the snow drift that had enveloped it: 'the hut shook and shivered, and we expected every minute to see our camp lifted bodily into the air like a balloon … we earnestly began to consider our chances, while now and again a jocular suggestion was passed from bunk to bunk as to how we should best be able to steer our hut in case it suddenly became an air-ship…'

While the scientific programme was maintained despite the conditions during the winter months, zoologist Nicolai Hanson died in October 1899 after a slow decline. The expeditioner's plans to explore Antarctica's interior the following summer had to be curtailed when they discovered a mountain range crossing their path. The party was picked up by the *Southern Cross* at the end of January 1900 and continued south into the Ross Sea towards the Ross Ice Shelf before turning for home.

Now restored by the New Zealand Antarctic Heritage Trust, Borchgrevink's huts stand as a reminder of the privations of early Antarctic explorers.

Carsten Borchgrevink's hut at Cape Adare. © Antarctic Heritage Trust, Christchurch, New Zealand

Plan of Carsten Borchgrevink's huts at Cape Adare. © Antarctic Heritage Trust, Christchurch, New Zealand

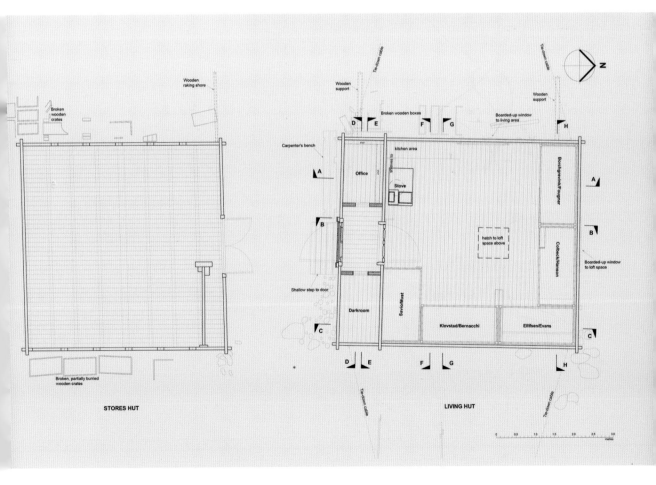

13

PRIMUS STOVE

Cold, hunger and dehydration are the worst enemies of Antarctic explorers, and no device has been more important in keeping those at bay than the Primus stove. First developed and patented in 1892 by a Swedish factory mechanic, Frans Wilhelm Lindqvist, Primus stoves are light and transportable pressurised kerosene burners. Made of brass, they consist of a fuel tank with a pump to pressurise the kerosene, a rising tube, and a burner assembly above which sits a metallic ring on which to set a pot.

Thanks to its reliability, lightness and ease of use, the Primus was for many decades the stove of choice for expeditions into icy environments. Among the many explorers and mountaineers who used Primuses were Fridtjof Nansen, Richard Byrd and George Mallory. Carsten Bochgrevink's *Southern Cross* expedition of 1898–1900 was the first to take Primus stoves to Antarctica, and they continue to be used today by many Antarctic field expeditions.

In the words of Roald Amundsen, leader of the first expedition to reach the South Pole: 'For cooking on sledge journeys the Primus stove ranks above all others; it gives a great deal of heat, uses little oil and requires no attention – advantages which are important enough anywhere, but especially when sledging. There is never any trouble with this apparatus; it has come as near perfection as possible.'

When problems did occur, the culprits were usually ancillaries or human errors – for example, when the matches required to light a Primus had got wet, or a lack of ventilation inside a tent led to sometimes deadly carbon monoxide poisoning. Kerosene was also known to 'creep' from tin containers in extremely cold temperatures. This was something Amundsen knew about from his experiences in the Arctic,

but Robert Falcon Scott did not anticipate and which contributed to his tragic end after the kerosene ran out.

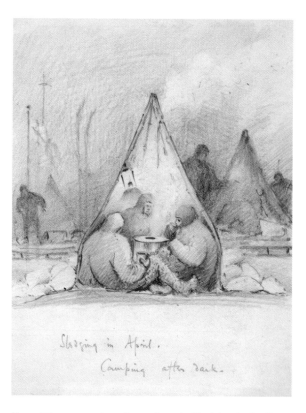

Men sitting around a primus stove in *Sledging in April. Camping after Dark.* By Edward Wilson, 1911.
© Scott Polar Research Institute, University of Cambridge, United Kingdom

Primus stove from the British Antarctic *Southern Cross* expedition of 1898–1900. Photo by Johannes van Kan.
© Antarctic Heritage Trust, Christchurch, New Zealand

When combined with a Nansen cooker, which replaced standard pots and combined a series of cylindrical aluminium vessels, a Primus stove could be used to simultaneously cook a meal in the central vessel, melt snow in the surrounding one, warm the tent and dry clothing hung from above. The Nansen cooker also halved the time required to cook or melt ice. Although dietary approaches differed between expeditions, meals cooked on a Primus most often consisted of wholemeal biscuit crushed into pemmican, a highly calorific mixture of dried red meat and fat. Once warmed, the melted snow was used to make tea or calorie-rich hot cocoa made by mixing chocolate, sugar and powdered milk. Comfort for body and soul.

14

HARNESS

Few objects are more emblematic of the glories and horrors of the Heroic Age of Antarctic exploration than the harnesses used by explorers to man-haul their heavily loaded sledges. This particular harness was designed by Robert Falcon Scott for his *Discovery* expedition of 1901–04, the first to journey deep into Antarctica's hinterland: travelling first across the Ross Ice Shelf in the direction of the South Pole, then west onto the Antarctic Plateau to claim Victoria Land and the South Magnetic Pole; and finally around Ross Island to Cape Crozier.

Confident of the advantages that his new harness design would bring to their endeavours, Robert Scott described the contraptions in this way: 'Each man had a broad band of webbing passing round his waist and supported by braces over the shoulders; the two ends of the band joined in an iron ring, to which a rope was attached which could be secured to the sledge or the trace. In the old days men were accustomed to pull from the shoulder, and thus of necessity assumed a somewhat lop-sided attitude; with our arrangement, by adjusting the braces the weight could be distributed very evenly over the upper part of the body, and this I believe made the pulling easier and gave greater freedom for breathing.'

Once in the field, however, man-hauling still proved torturous. Sledges were often overloaded with equipment and provisions, weighing up to 170kg (375lb) per man. Some days, the snow surface was so soft and sticky that despite the help received from sails fixed to the sledges, harnesses dug into the explorer's flesh and bones with every step. On such days, the distance travelled shrunk from 25km (15.5 miles) on a good day to just a couple of kilometres. In Scott's words: 'The sledge was like a log; two of us could scarcely move it, and therefore throughout the long hours we could none of us relax our efforts for a single moment — we were forced to keep a continuous strain on our harness with a tension that kept our ropes rigid and made conversation

A brown textile man-hauling harness used during the British National Antarctic *Discovery* Expedition, 1901–04. © Scott Polar Research Institute, University of Cambridge, United Kingdom

Dr Koettlitz, Bernacchi and the carpenter starting south-west. British National Antarctic *Discovery* Expedition, 1901–04. Photo by Reginald Skelton. © Scott Polar Research Institute, University of Cambridge, United Kingdom

quite impossible ... it is rather too much when the strain on the harness is so great, and we are becoming gaunt shadows of our former selves.'

One situation where harnesses were welcome, however, was when someone fell into a crevasse, as happened to Scott himself: 'I felt a violent blow on my right thigh, and all the breath seemed to be shaken out of my body. Instinctively I thrust out my elbows and knees, and then saw that I was

some little way down a crevasse ... my harness had held.' This time, Scott's harness saved his life, but a decade later the strain and hardship of man-hauling to the South Pole would contribute to his demise and that of his companions.

Despite the difficulties and hardships with which they are associated, harnesses remain an indispensable piece of equipment for anyone still wanting to pull sledges across Antarctica.

15

GAS BALLOON

The Deutsche Südpolar-Expedition, also known as the *Gauss* expedition, departed from the German port city of Kiel on 11 August 1901, intending to explore the lands lying south of the Kerguelen Islands. The expedition was led by Erich von Drygalski, a young professor of geophysics who had already been on two scientific expeditions to Greenland. The *Gauss* reached the Antarctic mainland on 21 February 1902, in a region christened Kaiser Wilhelm II Land. Shortly after their arrival, the ship was caught fast in the ice and thus became the expedition's base for the remainder of the expedition.

The *Gauss* expedition had an ambitious scientific programme. Using dog sledges, the men mapped hundreds of kilometres of territory, conducted geological studies at a large extinct volcano that they named Gaussberg, took geomagnetic and oceanographic measurements, and engaged in microbiological research. The men also gathered water and biological samples, discovering 1,430 new species in the process, further revealing the richness of life in Antarctic waters.

On 29 March 1902, taking advantage of good weather conditions, preparations were made for a manned balloon ascent near the ship. After filling their balloon with hydrogen, Drygalski made the first ascent, reaching a height of 50m (164ft). Two ascents followed, before an unpleasant turn in weather prompted the men to release the gas. Through their balloon ascents, the men were able to see far into the distance; scenes that revealed that Gaussberg was the only visible natural landmark.

Only two months earlier, British explorers from the *Discovery* expedition had also made a manned balloon flight, near Ross Island. The *Discovery* and *Gauss* expeditions contributed the first aerial photographs of the Antarctic continent, setting the precedent for future aerial

Manned balloon ascent on 29 March 1902 during the Deutsche Südpolar-Expedition, 1901–03. Photo by Emil Philippi. © Private collection of Volkert Gazert

Aerial view of the *Gauss* taken during the balloon ascent, 1902. © Private collection of Volkert Gazert

surveys, first from aeroplanes and later with satellites. These balloon flights were also the last time that Antarctica was seen from the air until 1928, when Australian explorer George Hubert Wilkins flew over a portion of the Antarctic Peninsula in his aeroplane, *San Francisco*.

After their return to Germany in 1903, Drygalski published 20 volumes and two atlases covering the scientific results of the expedition. Although this expedition was a major success from a scientific perspective, it was a political disappointment. While their British rivals had reached the highest southern latitude to date, Drygalski's men barely passed the Antarctic Circle. The continued rivalry between Germany and Britain set the stage for the 1911–13 Second German Antarctic Expedition, also known as the *Deutschland* expedition, which further demonstrated Germany's strength as an imperial power and also delivered important scientific results.

16

RIFLE

Unlike visitors to the Arctic, who can face life-threatening encounters with polar bears, the relative harmlessness of Antarctic fauna and the designation of the region as a continent for peace makes the necessity of weapons seem incongruous. Firearms, however, hold an important role in Antarctic history.

One of the primary purposes of firearms was hunting seabirds. On the *Southern Cross* expedition of 1898–1900, Carsten Borchgrevink described an incident when a crew member, unused to handling guns, fired on a petrel and hit zoologist Nicolai Hanson, 'who was taking sea temperatures, received a shower of the shot on his back and was not much pleased'. The 1901–03 Swedish Antarctic Expedition, led by Otto Nordenskjöld, lost their ship and survived off a diet of hunted seabirds while stranded on Paulet Island for nearly nine months before rescue.

In addition to birds, men used guns and other weapons to hunt seals and other animals well into the 20th century. Those hunting seals on a larger scale for their blubber used a combination

of lances, rifles and clubs. When hunting elephant seals in 1912, naturalist Robert Cushman Murphy observed that 'The big bulls are ... almost impossible to stop in their tracks unless a bullet pierces the parietal bone at the side of the brain case...'

Besides hunting Antarctic fauna, firearms were frequently used to kill dogs in the field, either as a supplement to the men's diet, because they were no longer useful, or because they consumed too much food. During Ernest Shackleton's 1914–17 *Endurance* expedition, dogs were primarily shot due to ailments early in the expedition and lack of supplies later. Following the sinking of the *Endurance*, three puppies and the carpenter's pet cat, Mrs Chippy, had to be shot, since 'We could not undertake

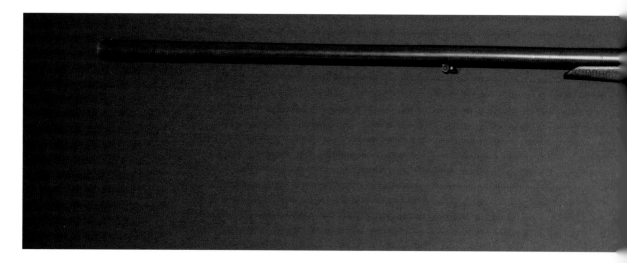

the maintenance of weaklings under the new conditions'. When the crew eventually shot the last teams, 'We had some of the dog-meat cooked, and it was not at all bad'.

During the 1911–14 Australasian Antarctic Expedition, Douglas Mawson and Xavier Mertz shot and ate their dogs after their teammate, Belgrave Edward Sutton Ninnis, fell into a crevasse with most of their supplies. Roald Amundsen's 1910–12 *Fram* expedition intentionally planned to shoot dogs and feed them to the men and other dogs. After killing superfluous animals at a site nicknamed 'the Butcher's Shop', Amundsen recalled that 'It had been arranged that we should stop here two days to rest and eat dog. There was more than one among us who at first would not hear of taking any part in this feast; but as time went by, and appetites became sharper, this view underwent a change, until, during the last few days before reaching the Butcher's Shop, we all thought and talked of nothing but dog cutlets, dog steaks, and the like.'

Environmental protection laws and cultural shifts have meant that firearms are no longer essential tools of Antarctic exploration, but they have not completely vanished from the greater Antarctic region. In fact, in the 2010s, the British government recruited hunters to cull the reindeer population on the subantarctic island of South Georgia, first introduced a century earlier to be hunted for food and recreation by Antarctic whalers.

The Antarctic Butcher, representing the killing of seals for dog food during the United States' Operation *Deep Freeze*. By Standish Backus, 1956. © Naval History and Heritage Command, Washington DC, United States

Single-barrelled rifle used during the Swedish Antarctic Expedition, 1901–03. © Grenna Museum Polarcenter, Gränna, Sweden

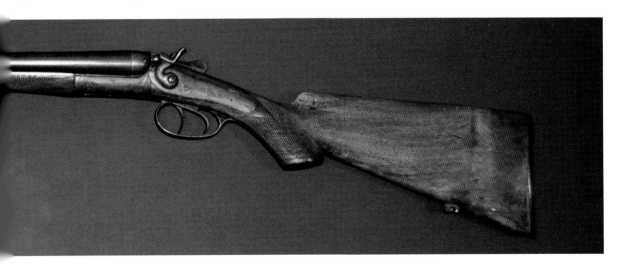

17

CHAMPAGNE

Even though the excessive consumption of alcohol has wreaked havoc in Antarctica as elsewhere, its importance is also accentuated by the isolation of Antarctic communities. Roald Amundsen, who was no fan of rowdiness, recognised its benefits: 'Personally, I regard alcohol, used in moderation, as a medicine in the Polar Regions'. Ernest Shackleton subscribed to the notion of alcohol as a physical and mental tonic, describing how it was usual to toast 'Absent Friends' and 'Sweethearts and Wives'.

This photograph shows Ernest Gourdon and Paul Pléneau, two members of Jean-Baptiste Charcot's first Antarctic expedition on board the *Français*, sharing a bottle of Mumm Cordon Rouge brut champagne to celebrate either Bastille Day 1904 or Charcot's birthday a day later, on 15 July. The photograph was also intended to promote Cordon Rouge as the 'Champagne of winners and aesthetes', the celebratory beverage of choice for Charcot and his crew.

The Mumm family were one of the sponsors of Charcot's first Antarctic expedition, providing it with both funds and plenty of bottles of Cordon Rouge. Charcot reciprocated by providing promotional photographs, but also by naming a small island to the north of Graham Land along the Antarctic Peninsula in honour of the family. Another example of 'Antarctic advertising' during the Heroic Age was Herbert Ponting's photograph of Frederick Hooper posing with an open can of Heinz baked beans during the *Terra Nova* expedition.

The use of Antarctica as a backdrop to advertise products continues to this day, often by brands that have little or no link to the continent or its history but find benefit in identifying with modern clichés about the purity, danger, fragility or exoticism of the Antarctic. These include Volkswagen and its Beetle automobile, Jaeger underwear, Diesel swimmers, Coca-Cola, Grape Nuts cereal, Kay Jewelers and Geico insurance policies.

Other brands, however, are more directly rooted in Antarctic history and culture. Watchmakers Rolex and Smiths have sponsored Antarctic expeditions and adventurers since the International Geophysical Year of 1957–58, and many of the suppliers of mountaineering and extreme sports equipment have associated their name with adventuring expeditions. Two brands, Amundsen Sports and Shackleton clothing, have gone a step further in naming themselves after legends of exploration, thus perpetuating the idea of Antarctica as a place for heroes and adventure.

In the realm of alcohol, among those that have extended Mumm's example are Glenfiddich Whisky, which sponsored a Walking with the Wounded Expedition in 2013, and Godet, which has distilled a special clear cognac labelled 'Antarctica Icy White'. Others have also adopted names associated with Antarctica, such as Amundsen Vodka, Scott Base Vineyard, Tom Crean Brewery, Antarctica Cerveja Pilsen, and the Süd Polaire, a triple distilled gin made in Tasmania.

Ernest Gourdon and Paul Pléneau sharing a bottle of Mumm champagne on 14/15 July 1904, Jean-Baptiste Charcot's birthday. Photo by Ernest Gourdon. © Courtesy of G. H. Mumm & Cie, Reims, France

The most famous, however, is Shackleton Whisky, a brand inspired by the 2010 discovery of three crates of Mackinlay's Rare Old Highland Malt Whisky at Cape Royds, Shackleton's hut during the *Nimrod* expedition of 1907–09. Three bottles were sent to Whyte & Mackay, the current owners of the Mackinlay brand, whose master blender created a replica that is still manufactured and commercialised around the world under the name Shackleton Whisky. Little remembered is the fact that Shackleton's last conversation before dying at the premature age of 47 was about him needing to cut back on his heavy drinking.

18

AURORA AUSTRALIS

Newspapers and magazines created by exploring expeditions have a long history in the Polar Regions. The first such publication created in Antarctica, was a monthly magazine to which all members of the 1901–04 *Discovery* expedition were invited to contribute. The result, edited by Ernest Shackleton and Louis Bernacchi, was a wonderfully eclectic evocation of the life of a small, isolated Antarctic community during the Edwardian period, called *Aurora Australis*.

Aurora Australis, 1908. © Jonkers Rare Books, Henley-on-Thames, United Kingdom

Known as the *South Polar Times*, this first Antarctic publication included humorous anecdotes, poems, scientific essays, weather reports and more. These were accompanied by photographic prints, cut-outs, drawings and watercolours depicting landscapes, fauna and the men. All artwork was original and texts were typewritten, meaning that there was only one copy of the *South Polar Times*, and that everyone had to take their turn to read it.

Having witnessed the popularity and benefits of the *South Polar Times* in boosting morale and staving off boredom, Shackleton chose to repeat the experience during the *Nimrod* expedition, which he led in 1907–09. This time, however, he added printing presses to the equipment taken south and chose to produce a single bound book instead of a monthly magazine. Donated by Joseph Causton & Sons, the printing and etching presses allowed the production of 70–100 copies of *Aurora Australis* (the exact number remains unknown).

Comprising texts by 9 of the 14 members of the expedition, as well as lithographs and etchings by artist George Marston, *Aurora Australis* was printed on Abbey Mills Greenfield paper, with the bindings fashioned out of an early form of plywood, Venesta board, recovered from the expedition cases. In his preface, Shackleton wrote that: 'During the sunless months which are now our portion; months lit only by vagrant aurora; we have found in this work an interest and a relaxation.'

The tradition of producing magazines and books continues at Antarctic stations to this day. Rare, however, are those with the authentic charm and

Cover of the *Halley Comet,* produced during the Royal Society Expedition to Halley Bay, 1958. By David Tribble. © British Antarctic Survey Archives Service, Cambridge, United Kingdom (ref. AD7/Z/1958/3)

beauty of the earliest ones. In fact, some from the second half of the 20th century comprise the kind of lewd material that was more prominent within male communities at the time.

At their best as at their worst, Antarctic publications reflect the enduring need to occupy the mind and maintain a sense of camaraderie while living in Antarctic isolation.

19

ANEMOMETER

Meteorological research has been important in the Antarctic since the earliest days of its exploration. To make meteorological observations, scientists depend on several instruments, including thermometers to measure air temperature, barometers to measure air pressure, and anemometers to measure wind velocity. An early example of an anemometer used in Antarctica was brought down by Jean-Baptiste Charcot during his second expedition to the Antarctic Peninsula in 1908–10 on board the *Pourquoi-Pas?* Anemometer readings also contributed to Douglas Mawson dubbing Cape Denison in East Antarctica 'the windiest place on Earth', during his 1911–14 Australasian Expedition.

The earliest permanent meteorological station in the Antarctic was established in 1903 by William Speirs Bruce on Laurie Island during the Scottish National Antarctic Expedition. Following Bruce's departure, the station was handed over to the Argentine government, which renamed it Orcadas in 1951. This station, still active today, is responsible for the longest continuous meteorological record in the Antarctic.

Servicio Meteorológico Nacional anemometer at Carlini Base in the South Shetland Islands, 2022. © Alfredo 'Alpio' Costa, Instituto Antártico Argentino, Buenos Aires, Argentina

After the Second World War, the rapid increase in permanent Antarctic research stations led to meteorological and atmospheric science becoming a constant of Antarctic research programmes. Motivated by their disputes over territorial sovereignty on the Antarctic Peninsula, Argentina, Chile and the United Kingdom built two dozen meteorological stations across the peninsula between 1944 and 1955. Their primary goal was to use their newly acquired expertise about the local environment, as well as their semi-permanent occupation to strengthen their respective claims to the region. Despite their political origins, these meteorological stations enabled scientists to assemble air temperature readings and other measurements that went on to serve as a baseline for modern studies in weather and climate, including studies of climate change and global warming.

One important discovery resulting from continuous meteorological recordings was the phenomenon of wind chill, the lowering of body temperature due to the passing flow of lower-temperature air. The first wind chill formulas and tables were developed by American geographer Paul Siple and palaeontologist Charles Passel during the United States Antarctic Service

Anemometer used during Jean-Baptiste Charcot's *Pourquoi-Pas?* expedition, 1908–10. © Frédéric Perin, Météo France, Saint-Mandé, France

Expedition, 1939–41. According to Siple, 'it becomes apparent to anyone subjected to cold that a windy day feels much colder than a calm day on which the temperature may actually register a considerably lower temperature. I adopted the word "wind-chill" to express this factor, recognising that it was in reality a rate at which the body was cooling.'

Siple and Passel based their tables on a set of experiments studying the cooling rate of a small plastic bottle as its contents turned to ice while suspended in the wind on the expedition hut roof, at the same level as a thermometer and an anemometer. Their models were widely used through the end of the century.

While many scientific instruments in Antarctica have become increasingly sophisticated, the ubiquity of traditional instruments like thermometers, barometers and anemometers demonstrates how even with scientific questions changing, some means of gathering data have remained the same.

20

CANARY

The Polar Regions are often referred to as 'the canary in the coal mine': environments at the front line of climate change. Fittingly, standing on the piano in Roald Amundsen's home in Uranienborg, Norway, is a beautiful but lifeless yellow canary. Named after Amundsen's mentor Fridtjof Nansen, Fridtjof was presented as a gift to Amundsen's expedition and is almost certainly the only canary to have travelled south of the Antarctic Circle.

Fridtjof departed Norway on board the *Fram* on 9 August 1910. Initially bound for the North Pole, the expedition changed course after Amundsen announced to his men that as Robert Peary and Frederick Cook had recently declared their independent conquests of the North Pole, he would now attempt to be the first to reach 90° South.

Although the canary remained on board when Amundsen disembarked at the Bay of Whales in 1911, Fridtjof returned to Antarctica in January 1912 as the *Fram* (which had spent the interim carrying out oceanographic work in the South Atlantic) sailed back to pick up the triumphant Amundsen. According to the ship's first lieutenant, Thorvald Nilsen, Fridtjof provided much entertainment: 'After dinner we enjoyed our usual Sunday cigar, while the canary, which has become Kristensen's pet, and hangs in his cabin, sang at the top of its voice.'

When Fridtjof eventually perished during the *Fram*'s return to Norway, the expedition's cook, Adolf Lindstrøm, prepared and presented the taxidermy of the canary to Amundsen.

Although a pioneer of its kind, Fridtjof was certainly not the first or only pet to journey to Antarctica. For a start, since rats were ever present on board ships, cats were often found,

both as pets and pest controls. They are recorded on board James Clark Ross' *Erebus* and *Terror* as early as 1839–43. Perhaps the most famous cat

IGLOO

A sketch of Richard Byrd's dog, Igloo, in his signature jacket and booties. By Elsie Miller, *c*.1930. © Byrd Polar and Climate Research Center Archival Program, The Ohio State University, Columbus, United States

Taxidermy of Fridtjof, the canary that travelled to
Antarctica on board Roald Amundsen's *Fram*.
© Museene i Akershus, Uranienborg, Norway

was Mrs Chippy, one of two felines on board the
Endurance, who despite the protests of its owner,
Harry McNish, was sacrificed by Shackleton after
the ship was sunk by the pack ice. Cats also found
their place in station life right up until the 1990s,
when non-native species (with the exception of
humans) were banned from Antarctica by the
Protocol on Environmental Protection to the
Antarctic Treaty.

Dogs are of course also omnipresent in Antarctic
history, but the vast majority were taken south to
pull sledges, not as pets. One notable exception
was Richard Byrd's dog Igloo, a white fox terrier
that joined Byrd's first Antarctic expedition

in 1928–30. Other pets that have made it to
Antarctica include rabbits, hamsters, guinea pigs
and Jean-Baptiste Charcot's pet pig, Toby, taken
south in 1904.

Like most dogs, ponies, mules and even alpacas
were taken to Antarctica to pull sledges, although
the latter were killed by dogs en route. Animals
have also been taken to Antarctica for food.
During his second Antarctic expedition (1933–35),
Richard Byrd took two Guernsey cows to provide
milk, but also for publicity and the geopolitical
flex that comes from successful agriculture. In
the 1960s, Chilean naval personnel operated an
experimental breeding programme at Captain
Arturo Prat Base, where they kept cattle, sheep
and pigs as sources of fresh meat. Although
perhaps not as charming as a canary, they too
were Antarctic pioneers.

21

EYE PROTECTION

Along with frostbite and sunburn, snow blindness and the intense agony it can cause is one of the most recurrent afflictions experienced by those who took part in the early history of polar exploration, especially during sledging journeys.

While people have been experimenting with devices to protect their eyes from the glare of the sun since ancient times, it is the Indigenous peoples of the Arctic that, since prehistory, have maintained the most enduring tradition of using eye protection devices. In most cases, these consisted of bone, ivory or wooden eye-coverings that only allow light to penetrate through a narrow horizontal strip, thus protecting the eyes from sun, wind and drift, but also significantly reducing the vertical field of vision of anyone wearing them.

Glass spectacles used by Roald Amundsen during his *Fram* expedition, 1910–12. © Vestfold Museums, Norway

Arctic-inspired snow goggles made during Roald Amundsen's *Fram* expedition, 1910–12. © Vestfold Museums, Norway

The effort to combine eye protection with clear vision eventually led to experiments with tinted glass, but it was only during the interwar period that modern sunglasses able to block ultraviolet light started to become more widespread. Most Antarctic expeditions prior to the First World War thus had to satisfy themselves with a whole variety of experimental eye protection. Since Indigenous Arctic eyewear had been successful in the frozen north, many Antarctic explorers adopted this technology for their own use.

The Antarctic-inspired goggles shown here were produced by Olav Bjaaland during Roald Amundsen's Antarctic expedition of 1910–12. In Amundsen's own words: 'Novelties in the way of snow-goggles were many. This was, of course, a matter of the greatest importance and required study – it was studied, too! The particular problem was to find good goggles without glass. It is true that I had worn nothing but a pair of ordinary spectacles, with light yellow glasses, all

the autumn, and that they had proved excellent; but for the long journey I was afraid these would give insufficient protection. I therefore threw myself into the competition for the best patent. The end of it was that we all went in for leather goggles, with a little slit for the eyes. The Bjaaland patent won the prize, and was most adopted.'

Amundsen had based his own model on a patent by American explorer Frederick Cook that was also based on Inuit design, but ultimately found that despite his original reservations, it was indeed his yellow glass spectacles that ended up giving him the best protection during the return journey to the South Pole: 'The spectacles I wore – Hanssen had the same; they were the only two pairs we had – gave perfect protection; not once did I have a sign of snow-blindness … Dr. Schanz, of Dresden, who sent me these glasses, has every right to be satisfied with his invention; it beats anything I have ever tried or seen.'

22

SKIS

The importance of skis in the early history of Antarctic exploration is hard to overstate. In the words of Roald Amundsen, leader of the first expedition to reach the South Pole: 'Every day we had occasion to bless our skis. We often used to ask each other where we should now have been without these excellent appliances. The usual answer was: Most probably at the bottom of some crevasse … it was clear to all of us, who were born and bred with ski on our feet, that these must be regarded as indispensable. This view was confirmed and strengthened every day, and I am not giving too much credit to our excellent skis when I say that they not only played a very important part, but possibly the most important of all, on our journey to the South Pole. Many a time we traversed stretches of surface so cleft and disturbed that it would have been an impossibility to get over them on foot. I need scarcely insist on the advantages of skis in deep, loose snow.'

Amundsen's success with skis was in no small part thanks to his own foresight in anticipating this kind of terrain, going as far as designing and ordering special skis measuring 2.5m (8.2ft), or somewhere between the length of cross-country and jumping skis. So important were skis to the expedition's success that at the end of each day, the men were ordered to detach their bindings and to store them safely inside their tent. The leather bindings had been strengthened to withstand the extreme stress of the Antarctic environment and Amundsen feared that they would be devoured by the ravenous dogs.

The main difficulty with skis, however, was knowing how to get the most out of them for speed and to preserve energy. While the Norwegians were experts at this, their British counterparts proved amateurs at best, and for the most part only learned how to use them once they had arrived in Antarctica.

The skis shown here belonged to Olav Bjaaland, a champion skier, carpenter and violinist from Telemark, the cradle of modern skiing, whose

abilities and character led to an invitation to join Amundsen's expedition. One of the best skiers in Norway, Bjaaland had previously won the Nordic combined at the Holmenkollen Ski Festival, among the classic events of Nordic skiing, and in many ways regarded Amundsen's bid to be the first at the South Pole as just another ski race. Bjaaland was often used as the front runner during the journey so that the dogs had someone to run after. Again in Amundsen's words: 'Going in front of the dogs up these slopes was, I could see, a business that Bjaaland would accomplish far more satisfactorily than I, and I gave up the place to him. … It was a pleasure to watch [him] use his ski up there.'

Even with the advent of the mechanical age, skis continued to be used in Antarctica. In 1946, American explorer Finn Ronne, whose father Martin Ronne had accompanied Amundsen to Antarctica, charted more than 5,700km (3,542 miles) on ski and sledge, more than any explorer in history. Today, skis are mostly employed by adventure tourists and participants in re-enactments of Heroic Age expeditions.

Olav Bjaaland's skis used on the trek to the South Pole during Roald Amundsen's *Fram* expedition, 1910–12.
© Ski Museum, Oslo, Norway

23

SPONSORSHIP SOLICITATION

In the first two decades of the 20th century, several countries launched expeditions to explore Antarctica. While some European expeditions have received more attention, other explorers were interested in making their mark on the Antarctic landscape. One such explorer was the Imperial Japanese Army officer Nobu Shirase.

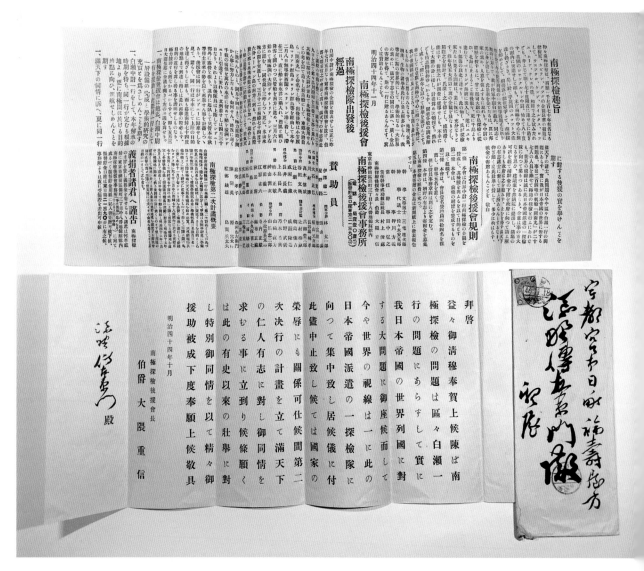

Solicitation mailing from the Society for the Support of the Japanese Antarctic Expedition, 1911.
© Chet Ross Rare Books, Tucson, United States

Before turning his attention to the Antarctic, Shirase had long nursed ambitions to lead an expedition to the North Pole. In 1893–95 he was a member of the *Chishima* expedition, which attempted to establish a permanent Japanese colony on the northernmost of the Kuril Islands. Although this expedition went badly, Shirase was not deterred. After fighting in the Russo-Japanese War of 1904–05, Shirase's plan to be the first to lead an expedition to the North Pole was aborted when Americans Frederick Cook and Robert Peary independently claimed precedence in reaching it.

Group photograph of the members of the Japanese Antarctic Expedition, 1911. Nobu Shirase sitting in the centre of the front row. © *Scottish Geographical Magazine*, 27:3, 1911

Instead, Shirase immediately began to search for sponsorship for a small Antarctic expedition. While he did not get financial support from the government, he was endorsed by the influential former prime minister Shigenobu Okuma, who proclaimed that 'such a heroic enterprise was unprecedented in the annals of Japan'. This helped Shirase gain private support, mostly in the form of small donations. In November 1910, Shirase and his crew of 27 volunteers sailed south on board a retrofitted fishing vessel, named the *Kainan Maru* (Southern Pioneer). They planned to arrive in Antarctica in early 1911, establish a winter base, and march to the South Pole in the summer of 1911–12.

Unfortunately, Shirase had departed too late. After facing terrible storms between New Zealand and Antarctica, the ship was endangered by pack ice and forced to head back north and wait out the winter in Sydney. Two men, Naokichi Nomura and Keiichi Tada, returned to Japan to try to raise more funds for their expedition and issued the solicitation shown here, dated 18 November 1911. It reminded the Japanese public that no one had yet reached the South Pole, before posing the question: 'To accomplish this worldwide, scientific, and splendid achievement, would you support us?'

While he was in Australia, Shirase changed the goals of his expedition. Since Amundsen and Scott now had a significant head start, he announced that rather than trying to plant the Japanese flag at the South Pole, he would explore as much of the Antarctic continent as he could within one season.

In January 1912, the *Kainan Maru* landed parties at the Great Ice Barrier in the Ross Sea, where they took meteorological observations, and on King Edward VII Land, where they gathered geological specimens. Shirase and a team of four men also launched an incursion into the interior, becoming the fourth Antarctic party to reach 80° South. The expedition left Antarctica and headed back to Tokyo in February 1912.

Although Shirase and his men received little fanfare on their return, they had achieved much during their limited time in Antarctica, making notable contributions to scientific research, geographical discovery and polar navigation.

24

PENGUIN EGGS

Robert Falcon Scott's 1910–13 *Terra Nova* expedition is most widely remembered for its ill-fated quest to be the first to reach the South Pole, but it was also a significant scientific enterprise, whose programme of research was led by the zoologist Edward Wilson.

Wilson decided that it would be a major contribution to science if the expedition could collect the embryo of an emperor penguin in order to test the theory that there existed a link between an organism's embryo development and its evolutionary history. The difficulty, however, was that emperors only breed in winter. In order to secure an unhatched egg, a group of three men, comprising Wilson, Henry Robertson Bowers and Apsley Cherry-Garrard, set out in the frozen darkness of the Antarctic winter and man-hauled two sledges weighing 180kg (397lb) each

Edward Wilson, Henry Robertson, Bowers and Apsley Cherry-Garrard on their return from their winter journey to Cape Crozier. Photo by Herbert Ponting, 1911. © Getty Images/Royal Geographical Society

from their wintering hut at Cape Evans to the nearest emperor rookery at Cape Crozier.

It took the party 19 days in temperatures that plummeted as low as -60°C (-76°F) to cover the 108km (67 miles) to Cape Crozier. In fact, they covered almost three times that distance as they went back and forth to haul the sledges one at a time. When they arrived, they built a stone shelter to carry out their ornithological work. After locating the emperor penguin rookery, they recovered eggs and adult penguins, which they used for both research and food. When a blizzard raged in, it blew away the team's tent and the canvas roof of their stone shelter. While they managed to recover the tent, they had to curtail their plans and set off back to Cape Evans with their precious treasure of five eggs. Having overcome unimaginable miseries, they reached Cape Evans 35 days later. Two of the eggs had broken during the return journey, but the three surviving ones were carefully cut open and the embryos removed and preserved.

In his classic account of the expedition, *The Worst Journey in the World* (1922), Cherry-Garrard wrote that 'Antarctic exploration is seldom as bad as you imagine, seldom as bad as it sounds. But this journey had beggared our language: no words could express its horror…' Despite their suffering, however, the men felt that their journey was worth it: 'After indescribable effort and hardship we were

Three emperor penguin eggs collected at Cape Crozier during the winter journey.
Photo by Herbert Ponting, 1911. © Getty Images/Royal Geographical Society

witnessing a marvel of the natural world, and we were the first and only men who had ever done so; we had within our grasp material which might prove of the utmost importance to science; we were turning theories into facts with every observation we made.'

Wilson and 'Birdie' Bowers later perished with Scott on their return journey from the South Pole. Upon his return to Britain, Cherry-Garrard delivered the eggs and embryos to the Natural

History Museum in London, but study of the specimens was delayed by the First World War. Between collecting the eggs and their eventual examination in 1934, science had moved on and the theory of a link between an organism's embryonic development and its evolutionary history had been rejected. In terms of their scientific goals, their journey had been for nothing, but with the publication of *The Worst Journey in the World*, it resulted in one of the greatest adventure narratives of the 20th century.

25

CAMERA

In the earliest days of its exploration, images of Antarctica consisted of a handful of sketches, paintings and engravings. Only with the onset of photography and film were explorers able to expose Antarctica's wild splendour to the wider public. Despite the difficulty of operating cumbersome photographic equipment in harsh Antarctic conditions, the resulting images had such an impact that photography soon became an integral part of Antarctica's expeditionary culture.

Among the handful of photographers who brought back images of Antarctica before the onset of the First World War in 1914, most were amateurs whose primary roles were scientific, medical or exploratory – not photographic. The first professional photographer to journey to Antarctica with his cameras was Englishman Herbert Ponting.

Herbert Ponting and telephoto apparatus, Antarctica, 1910. © Getty Images/Royal Geographical Society

By the time Robert Falcon Scott invited Ponting to join his 1910–13 *Terra Nova* expedition, the self-proclaimed 'camera artist' was already renowned for his coverage of the 1904–05 Russo-Japanese War for *Harper's Weekly*, as well as for his photographs of Asia and Europe published in leading illustrated magazines. In Scott's mind, Ponting's photographs and film would not only serve to document the expedition and share Antarctica's sublime beauty with the widest possible audience, but they would also contribute to recovering expeditionary costs through selling film and photographic rights, as well as by organising lantern-slide lectures, exhibitions and screenings.

Having accepted the position, Ponting assembled a 'colossal photographic outfit' that comprised at least six photographic cameras and two movie cameras. The photographic cameras included everything from this Kershaw Soho 17.5 x 12.5cm (7 x 5in) glass-plate Reflex camera designed by Ponting himself, and which he referred to as the *multum in parvo* ('much in a little'), to far smaller pocket cameras that could take film rolls and were taken on sledging journeys by other expedition members, including by the South Pole party. His equipment also included an array of lenses, including a mammoth telephoto lens. To house all this gear and develop his negatives, Ponting set up a darkroom on board the *Terra Nova*, and later in the wintering hut at Cape Evans. In fact, the latter took up so much of the available space in the hat that Scott obliged Ponting to also sleep in it.

Although the dominant subject is the Antarctic wilderness, Ponting's nearly 2,000 photographs also include magnificent portraits of the men,

'Grotto in Berg, *Terra Nova* in distance, Taylor and Wright (interior), 5 January 1911'. Photo by Herbert Ponting. © Getty Images/Scott Polar Research Institute, University of Cambridge

as well as pictures of their ship, their work and their winter life. So often did his companions have to pose for Ponting that the activity became known as 'to pont'. All meticulously composed, the majority of Ponting's photographs combine classical canons with a romantic sensitivity that continues to influence Antarctic photography, of which the most iconic example is his 1911 'Grotto in Berg'.

26

PONY SNOWSHOE

Sailing from its last port of call in New Zealand, the 1910–13 *Terra Nova* expedition, led by Robert Falcon Scott, carried 34 dogs, 3 motorised sledges and 19 Manchurian ponies to assist in its effort to be the first party to reach the South Pole.

Ponies had already been used in Antarctica during Ernest Shackleton's *Nimrod* expedition of 1907–09, based on the prior assumption that 'compared with the dog, the pony is a far more efficient animal, one pony doing the work of at least ten dogs on the food allowance for ten

dogs, and travelling a longer distance in a day'. Ponies, however, required that vast amounts of hay be transported to Antarctica, whereas dogs could be fed on local seals. Moreover, despite their reputed resilience, the ponies proved ill-adapted to local conditions. Some poisoned

Pony snowshoe, used during the *Terra Nova* expedition, 1910–13.
© Scott Polar Research Institute, University of Cambridge, United Kingdom

'Ponies on the March, southern journey, Great Ice Barrier, 2 December 1911'. Photo by Robert Falcon Scott.
© Scott Polar Research Institute, University of Cambridge, United Kingdom

themselves by eating the salty volcanic sand around the wintering hut, and the remainder succumbed from the strain during Shackleton's southern journey.

Despite Shackleton's experience, however, Scott continued to believe that ponies would be more useful than dogs, especially if equipped with equine snowshoes. Used in Scandinavia for centuries, these were made from 'a circle of wire as a foundation, hooped round with bamboo, and with beckets of the same material', and were meant to prevent the animals from sinking into the soft snow. In practice, however, the ponies received very little training in their use and Lawrence Oates, who was responsible for the ponies' care, never 'had any faith in these shoes at all'.

As a result, snowshoes were left behind on the first sledging journeys to lay supply depots for the planned bid to reach the South Pole, and the ponies had a very difficult time moving through the snow. Scott described one particularly bad experience: 'It couldn't move, and with such struggles as it made it sank deeper till only its head and forelegs showed above the slush.' Due to these repeated difficulties, the men were handicapped in their task and the last depot was laid almost 64km (40 miles) short of their goal.

The snowshoes were eventually put to some use during the journey to the South Pole, with Scott musing that, under the right circumstances, 'There is no doubt that these snowshoes are *the* thing for ponies, and had ours been able to use them from the beginning they would have been very different in appearance at this moment.' By now, however, the ponies were so deteriorated and the environmental conditions so strenuous that the snowshoes could no longer make a difference. On 9 December 1911, just before reaching the Beardmore Glacier, 'the ponies were quite done, one and all'. Scott, therefore, ordered that they be shot and lamented 'Poor beasts! They have done wonderfully well considering the terrible circumstances under which they worked.'

27

BLACK FLAG

On 16 January 1912, Robert Falcon Scott, Edward Wilson, Edgar Evans, Henry Robertson Bowers and Lawrence Oates were within 15km (9.3 miles) of reaching the South Pole. It was two and a half months since they had left the expedition's hut at Cape Evans, and they had already journeyed some 1,400km (870 miles) on foot and on skis. They were hungry, frostbitten and exhausted, but still hopeful of being the first men to reach 90° South and, in Scott's words, 'to secure for the British Empire the honour of this achievement'.

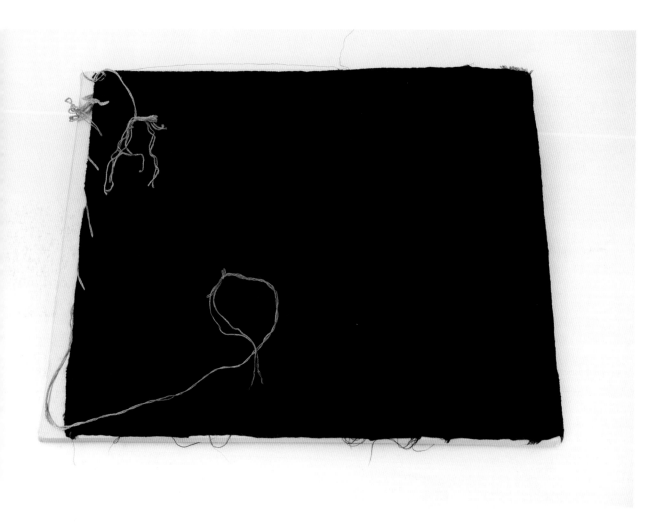

Black flag left by Roald Amundsen at the South Pole in December 1911. © Scott Polar Research Institute, University of Cambridge, United Kingdom

Then, as they approached the pole, 'The worst has happened, or nearly the worst ... Bowers' sharp eyes detected what he thought was a cairn; he was uneasy about it ... Half an hour later he detected a black speck ahead. Soon we knew that it could not be a natural snow feature. We marched on, found that it was a black flag tied to a sledge bearer; near the remains of a camp ... This told us the whole story. The Norwegians have forestalled us and are first at the Pole. It is a terrible disappointment, and I am very sorry for my loyal companions ... To-morrow we must march on to the Pole and then hasten home ...'

The flag in this picture is not the one described above but a second one, which they spotted two days later when, in Wilson's words: 'At our lunch South Pole camp we saw a sledge runner with a black flag about half a mile away bearing from it. Scott sent me on ski to fetch it and I found a note tied to it showing that this was the Norskies actual Pole position. I was given the flag and the note with Amundsen's signature and I got a piece of the sledge runner as well.'

Unlike the summit of a mountain, which is easily identifiable, the South Pole is an abstract location that, at the time and visually, remained un-differentiable from any other surrounding co-ordinate. The only way to locate it was by using a theodolite, sextant and artificial horizon, but exactitude remained almost impossible. According to Amundsen, 'every one of us knew that we were not standing on the absolute spot; it would be an impossibility with the time and the instruments at our disposal to ascertain that exact spot.'

To avoid any possible debate about his locating of the South Pole, or indeed any questioning his attainment, Amundsen took the precaution of framing it with another four black flags, each one planted some 20km (12.4 miles) away in opposing directions to form a square around the pole. This guaranteed that even if his calculation of the pole's position was questioned, no one could doubt that 90° South lay within the frame he had delineated. It was one of these four flags that was first spotted by 'Birdie' Bowers.

Heartbroken and already very weak, having reached the South Pole only to bear witness to Amundsen's success, Scott's party began their fateful journey back to Cape Evans. Later found among Wilson's belongings inside the tent in which he, Scott and Bowers died, Amundsen's South Pole black flag, once a symbol of their defeat, now seemed to embody their tragic end.

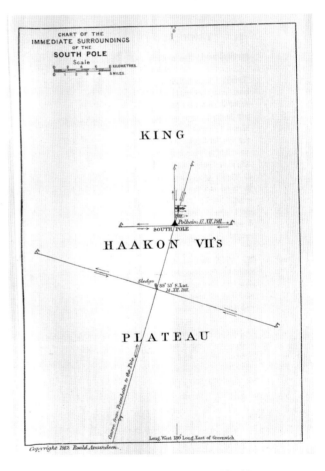

Roald Amundsen's chart of the flags planted by his party around the South Pole in 1911. © Roald Amundsen, *The South Pole*, 1913

28

FERN FOSSIL

While the ultimate goal of Robert Falcon Scott's South Pole Party was to be the first to reach 90° South, scientific exploration remained of the utmost importance, even as supplies were diminishing and the health of his party was deteriorating on their fateful return journey.

On 8 February 1912, Scott ordered his men to stop and gather fossils at the head of the Beardmore Glacier. He wrote: 'The moraine was obviously so interesting that when we had advanced some miles and got out of the wind, I decided to camp and spend the rest of the day geologising … We found ourselves under perpendicular cliffs of Beacon sandstone, weathering rapidly and carrying veritable coal seams. From the last Wilson, with his sharp eyes, has picked several plant impressions, the last a piece of coal with beautifully traced leaves in layers, also some excellently preserved impressions of thick stems, showing cellular structure.' The leaf impressions were specimens of *Glossopteris*, an extinct Permian fern. The men carried them all the way to their deaths and the fossils were eventually retrieved from alongside their bodies.

Geological research was immensely important to early Antarctic exploration. It was motivated as much by the possibility of coal and other mineral exploitation as by curiosity regarding the geological structure of this unknown territory. *Glossopteris* fossils took on a particular significance when German meteorologist Alfred Wegener began to advocate publicly for the idea of continental drift, arguing that all the continents were once joined together in a single landmass and had since drifted apart. In his 1915 book, *The Origin of Continents and Oceans*, Wegener relied heavily on the discover of *Glossopteris* fossils throughout the southern hemisphere as evidence that the continents had once been connected.

Alfred Wegener's *The Origin of Continents and Oceans,* 1922. © Courtesy of the Linda Hall Library of Science, Engineering and Technology, Kansas City, United States

Later geologists continued supporting continental drift using *Glossopteris* fossils as a key biogeographical component of their hypothesis. After the Commonwealth Trans-Antarctic Expedition of 1955–58, South African geologist Edna Plumstead argued that the *Glossopteris*

Fern fossils gathered during the *Terra Nova* expedition, 1910–13. © Scott Polar Research Institute, University of Cambridge, United Kingdom

fossils gathered during this expedition demanded 'a more plausible phytogeographical explanation than any given previously, and would appear to be satisfied only by the acceptance of some form of continental drift'.

Fossils such as these revealed that the Antarctic landscape was once lush and verdant prior to its break-up from the Gondwana supercontinent and final detachment from South America over 30 million years ago. Moreover, it was through studying these Antarctic fossils that many geologists changed our conception of the structure and evolution of the Earth itself.

29

DIARY

Presented and preserved alongside the greatest treasures of the British Library in London, including Shakespeare's First Folio, the original score of Handel's *Messiah* and the Magna Carta, no Antarctic diary is as renowned as Robert Falcon Scott's.

Daily diaries were common among polar explorers. Expeditioners were aware that accounts of their experiences could have monetary value in the future. Diaries also served as records and keepsakes for their loved ones. Additionally, different diaries could be pieced together into official accounts for the purposes of reconstructing the geography or scientific programmes of expeditions. Finally, as days ran together, diaries became a means of differentiation. As Apsley Cherry-Garrard, one of the other great literary voices of Antarctic exploration, put it: 'A diary in this life is one of the only ways in which a man can blow off steam.'

It is in part through Scott's diary that we can reconstruct the daily activities of the 1910–13 *Terra Nova* expedition, revealing their busy schedules, making camp, engaging in scientific observations and preparing for their field expeditions. Scott also documented the march to and from the South Pole, marked by exhausting labour, the death of their ponies and strategic changes in planning.

The most poignant passages in the diary are his recording of the deaths of his men on the return journey. Particularly moving was his account of the death of Lawrence Oates, who had suffered terrible frostbite in his feet. According to Scott, Oates intentionally walked into a blizzard and was never seen again. His last words were: 'I am just going outside and may be some time.' Scott characterised Oates' death as suicide, sacrificing himself so that the other three party members would have a chance to live: 'we knew it was the act of a brave man and an English gentleman.'

On 29 March 1912, Scott wrote his last entry, pleading for those who discovered the bodies of Edward Wilson, Henry Robertson Bowers and himself to take care of their respective families: 'It seems a pity, but I do not think I can write more. R. SCOTT. For God's sake look after our people.'

Knowing that his diary might be used to reconstruct the men's last days and shape the expedition's legacy, he also left a message to the public, explaining their party's failures and setting the ground for their later patriotic heroisation: 'We are weak, writing is difficult, but for my own sake I do not regret this journey, which has shown that Englishmen can endure hardships, help one another, and meet death with as great a fortitude as ever in the past. We took risks, we knew we took them; things have come out against us, and therefore we have no cause for complaint, but bow to the will of Providence, determined still to do our best to the last ... Had we lived, I should have had a tale to tell of the hardihood, endurance, and courage of my companions which would have stirred the heart of every Englishman. These rough notes and our dead bodies must tell the tale, but surely, surely, a great rich country like ours will see that those who are dependent on us are properly provided for.'

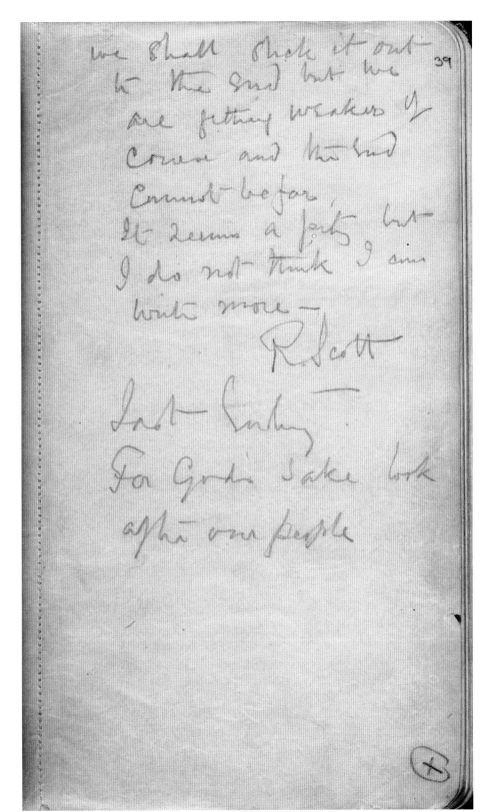

The last entry of Robert Falcon Scott's diary, 29 March 1912. © British Library Board, London, United Kingdom

30

HALF SLEDGE

The celebrated Australian explorer Douglas Mawson first travelled to Antarctica as a member of Ernest Shackleton's *Nimrod* expedition of 1907–09. On this expedition, Mawson was a member of the party that was the first to climb to the summit of Mount Erebus and to reach the Magnetic South Pole.

Upon his return, Mawson was invited to join Scott's 1910–13 *Terra Nova* expedition, but opted instead to organise his own expedition to King George V Land and Adélie Land in East Antarctica with the object of carrying out geographical exploration and scientific studies. The 1911–14 Australasian Antarctic Expedition departed from Australia in December 1911. Upon arrival, the crew established two bases, spending the first winter at Cape Denison where there were nearly constant blizzards and winds reaching speeds of over 300km/h (186mph).

In November 1912, the expedition broke into seven parties in order to survey the region and collect measurements and specimens. Mawson was part of the Far Eastern Party, intended to investigate previously unexplored territory of the Antarctic west of Cape Adare. This party also included British Army officer Belgrave Edward Sutton Ninnis and Swiss skier Xavier Mertz. The men travelled about 500km (310 miles) from camp, using sledge dogs to increase their speed.

On 14 December 1912, Ninnis, his dogs and his supply-laden sledge fell into a crevasse and were lost. Mertz and Mawson turned back west, killing the remaining sledge dogs for food as they travelled. About halfway back, Mertz became extremely ill and died a week later. It has been hypothesised that his cause of death was vitamin A poisoning from eating too much dog liver.

In the Blizzard at Cape Denison. Photo by Frank Hurley, 1913. © Getty Images/ullstein bild Dtl.

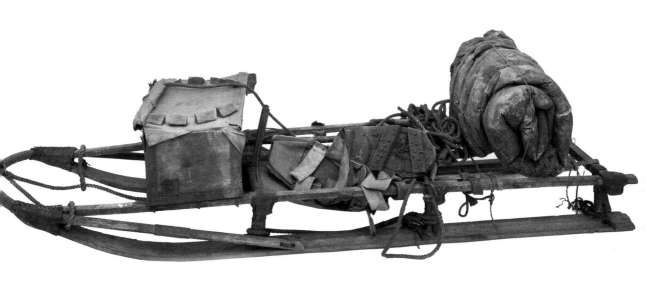

Half sledge man-hauled by Douglas Mawson on his return to Cape Denison.
© Royal Geographical Society, London, United Kingdom

Now alone, Mawson suffered from malnourishment and severe frostbite. He partially deconstructed his sledge, sawing it in half to lighten his load, then cooked and packed up the remaining dog meat, tied his sledge around his waist, and began man-hauling. On 17 January, it was his turn to fall into a crevasse, but he saved himself by climbing the rope anchored to his sledge. In early February, he reached Aladdin's Cave, a food depot 8.9km (5.5 miles) from Cape Denison. There he stayed for a week, trapped by a blizzard.

When Mawson arrived on base on 8 February 1913, he found that he had missed the ship back to Australia by only a few hours, but that relief parties had been left behind at Cape Denison

and the Western Base. Mawson remained with them in Antarctica for another eventful winter, during which the radio operator, Sidney Jeffryes, experienced a mental breakdown. Jeffryes was diagnosed with paranoid schizophrenia shortly after their return to Australia.

Despite the tragedies suffered by the Australasian Antarctic Expedition, the men carried out among the most expansive scientific programme of any expedition in the era, even discovering the first meteorite on the continent and mapped over 4,000km (2,485 miles) of unexplored territory. Mawson later led the British Australia New Zealand Antarctic Research Expedition in 1929–31, which resulted in the formation of the Australian Antarctic Territory in 1933.

31

PAGE FROM THE *ENCYCLOPAEDIA BRITANNICA*

The first *Encyclopaedia Britannica* to reach the shores of Antarctica was Cambridge University Press' renowned 11th edition, taken south by Douglas Mawson during his Australasian Antarctic Expedition of 1911–14. Donated by the philanthropist Campbell Mackellar, it contained 40,000 article headings in 28 volumes, plus an index.

Two sets of the same edition were donated to Ernest Shackleton's 1914–17 Imperial Trans-Antarctic Expedition. The first was gifted to the expedition's Ross Sea Party by John King Davis, master of their ship, the *Aurora*. The second was donated by Frank Bickerton, Mawson's mechanic during the Australasian Expedition, and was kept in Shackleton's cabin on board the *Endurance*. It was an extremely generous gift, especially from someone of modest means like Bickerton.

Having spent two winters in Antarctica, Shackleton appreciated more than most the value of reading to stave off boredom, or, in the words of Ross Sea Party member Richard W Richards, how 'most were content to accept the authority of the *Encyclopaedia Britannica* in settling an argument'. The men made extensive use of the *Encyclopaedia* during their wintering on board the ice-beset *Endurance*. Shackleton himself read extensively about the Assyrians, the Babylonians and the excavation of ancient monuments.

On 27 October 1915, when the time had come to abandon ship and set up camp on the sea ice, quick decisions had to be made about what to salvage. Food, warmth and shelter were the priority, but Shackleton felt that reading material was also essential. His diary entry from 3 November lists *Encyclopaedia Britannica* and the Queen's Bible as salvaged. Other members list volumes such as the *Iliad* and *Anna Karenina*.

Ernest Shackleton's cabin on the *Endurance*. Photo by Frank Hurley, 1914. © Getty Images/Royal Geographical Society

Despite their popularity, volumes of the *Encyclopaedia* eventually had to be abandoned to save weight as they moved camps, though the salvaged texts 'were the greatest treasure in the library'. By the time they reached Elephant Island and Shackleton sailed to South Georgia in search of rescue, just a few volumes remained. In the words of Thomas Orde-Lees, one of 23 men left behind to await rescue: 'I read so slowly that I shall never be able to read all that the volumes contain even if we have to stop here for five years which God forbid.'

Eventually, as weeks turned into months of waiting, the last volumes were rationed and pages began to be ripped out for needs more

(ib., 1867), and *Church Vestments* (ib., 1868); M. Dreger, *Künstlerische Entwicklung der Weberei und Stickerei* (Vienna, 1904); Madame I. Errera, *Collection de broderies anciennes* (Brussels, 1905); L. de Farcy, *La Broderie* (Paris, 1890); R. Forrer, *Die Gräber und Textilfunde von Achmim-Panopolis* (Strassburg, 1891); F. R. Fowke, *The Bayeux Tapestry* (London, 1898); Rev. C. H. Hartshorne, *On English Medieval Embroidery* (ib., 1848); M. B. Huish, *Samplers and Tapestry Embroideries* (ib., 1900); A. F. Kendrick, *English Embroidery* (ib., 1905); *English Embroidery executed prior to the Middle of the 16th Century* (Burlington Fine Arts Club Exhibition, 1905, introduction by A. F. Kendrick); E. Lefebure, *Embroideries and Lace*, translated by A. S. Cole, C.B. (London, 1888); F. Marshall, *Old English Embroidery* (ib., 1894); E. M. Rogge, *Moderne Kunst-Nadelarbeiten* (Amsterdam, 1905); South Kensington Museum, *Catalogue of Special Loan Exhibition of Decorative Art Needlework* (1874); W. G. P. Townshend, *Embroidery* (London, 1899). For further examples of ecclesiastical embroidery see the articles CHASUBLE, COPE, DALMATIC and MITRE. (A. F. K.; A. S. C.)

EMBRUN, a town in the department of the Hautes Alpes in S.E. France. It is built at a height of 2854 ft. on a plateau that rises above the right bank of the Durance. It is 27½ m. by rail from Briançon and 24 m. from Gap. Its ramparts were demolished in 1884. In 1906 the communal pop. (including the garrison) was 3752. Besides the Tour Brune (11th century) and the old archiepiscopal palace, now occupied by government offices, barracks, &c., the chief object of interest in Embrun is its splendid cathedral church, which dates from the second half of the 12th century. Above its side door, called the *Réal*, there existed till 1585 (when it was destroyed by the Huguenots) a fresco, probably painted in the 13th century, representing the Madonna; this was the object of a celebrated pilgrimage for many centuries. Louis XI. habitually wore on his hat a leaden image of this Madonna, for which he had a very great veneration, since between 1440 and 1461, during the lifetime of his father, he had been the dauphin, and as such ruler of this province.

Embrun was the *Eburodunum* or *Ebredunum* of the Romans, and the chief town of the province of the Maritime Alps. The episcopal see was founded in the 4th century, and became an archbishopric about 800. In 1147 the archbishops obtained from the emperor Conrad III. very extensive temporal rights, and the rank of princes of the Holy Roman Empire. In 1232 the county of the Embrunais passed by marriage to the dauphins of Viennois. In 1791 the archiepiscopal see was suppressed, the region being then transferred to the diocese of Gap, so that the once metropolitan cathedral church is now simply a parish church. The town was sacked in 1585 by the Huguenots and in 1692 by the duke of Savoy. Henri Arnaud (1641-1721), the Waldensian pastor and general, was born at Embrun.

See A. Albert, *Histoire du diocèse d'Embrun* (2 vols., Embrun, 1783); M. Fornier, *Histoire générale des Alpes Maritimes ou Cottiennes et particulière de leur métropolitaine Embrun* (written 1626-1643), published by the Abbé Paul Guillaume (3 vols., Paris and Gap, 1890-1891); A. Fabre, *Recherches historiques sur le pèlerinage des rois de France à N. D. d'Embrun* (Grenoble, 1859); A. Sauret, *Essai historique sur la ville d'Embrun* (Gap, 1860). (W. A. B. C.)

EMBRYOLOGY. The word embryo is derived from the Gr. ἔμβρυον, which signified the fruit of the womb before birth. In its strict sense, therefore, embryology is the study of the intrauterine young or embryo, and can only be pursued in those animals in which the offspring are retained in the uterus of the mother until they have acquired, or nearly acquired, the form of the parent. As a matter of fact, however, the word has a much wider application than would be gathered from its derivation. All animals above the Protozoa undergo at the beginning of their existence rapid growth and considerable changes of form and structure. During these changes, which constitute the development of the animal, the young organism may be incapable of leading a free life and obtaining its own food. In such cases it is either contained in the body of the parent or it is protruded and lies quiescent within the egg membranes; or it may be capable of leading an independent life, possessing in a functional condition all the organs necessary for the maintenance of its existence. In the former case the young organism is called an *embryo*,[1] in the latter a *larva*. It might thus be

[1] In the mammalia the word *foetus* is often employed in the same signification as embryo; it is especially applied to the embryo in the later stages of uterine development.

concluded that embryology would exclude the study of larvae, in which the whole or the greater part of the development takes place outside the parent and outside the egg. But this is not the case; embryology includes not only a study of embryos as just defined, but also a study of larvae. In this way the scope of the subject is still further widened. As long as embryology confines its attention to embryos, it is easy to fix its limits, at any rate in the higher animals. The domain of embryology ceases in the case of viviparous animals at birth, in the case of oviparous animals at hatching; it ceases as soon as the young form acquires the power of existing when separated from the parent, or when removed from the protection of the egg membranes. But as soon as post-embryonic developmental changes are admitted within the scope of the subject, it becomes on close consideration difficult to limit its range. It must include all the developmental processes which take place as a result of sexual reproduction. A man at birth, when he ceases to be an embryo, has still many changes besides those of simple growth to pass through. The same remark applies to a young frog at the metamorphosis. A chick even, which can run about and feed almost immediately after hatching, possesses a plumage very different from that of the full-grown bird; a starfish at the metamorphosis is in many of its features quite different from the form with which we are familiar. It might be attempted to meet this difficulty by limiting embryology to a study of all those changes which occur in the organism before the attainment of the adult state. But this merely shifts the difficulty to another quarter, and makes it necessary to define what is meant by the adult state. At first sight this may seem easy, and no doubt it is not difficult when man and the higher animals alone are in question, for in these the adult state may be defined comparatively sharply as the stage of sexual maturity. After that period, though changes in the organism still continue, they are retrogressive changes, and as such might fairly be excluded from any account of development, which clearly implies progression, not retrogression. But, as so often happens in the study of organisms, formulae which apply quite satisfactorily to one group require modifications when others are considered. Does sexual maturity always mark the attainment of the adult state? Is the Axolotl adult when it acquires its reproductive organs? Can a larval Ctenophore, which acquires functional reproductive glands and still possesses the power of passing into the form ordinarily described as adult in that group, be considered to have reached the end of its development? Or—to take the case of those animals, such as *Amphioxus*, *Balanoglossus*, and many segmented worms in which important developmental processes occur, *e.g.* formation of new gill slits, of gonadial sacs, or even of whole segments of the body, long after the power of reproduction has been acquired—how is the attainment of the adult state to be defined, for it is clear that in them the attainment of sexual maturity does not correspond with the end of growth and development? If, then, embryology is to be regarded as including not only the study of embryos, but also that of larvae, *i.e.* if it includes the study of the whole developmental history of the individual—and it is impossible to treat the subject rationally unless it is so regarded—it becomes exceeding difficult to fix any definite limit to the period of life with which embryology concerns itself. The beginning of this period can be fixed, but not the end, unless it be the end of life itself, *i.e.* death. The science of embryology, then, is the science of individual development, and includes within its purview all those changes of form and structure, whether embryonic, larval or post-larval, which characterize the life of the individual. The beginning of the period is precise and definite—it is the completion of the fertilization of the ovum, in which the life of the individual has its start. The end, on the other hand, is vague and cannot be precisely defined, unless it be death, in which case the period of life with which embryology concerns itself is coincident with the life of the individual. To use the words of Huxley ("Cell Theory," *Collected Works*, vol. i, p. 267): "Development, therefore, and life are, strictly speaking, one thing, though we are accustomed to limit the former to the progressive half of life merely, and

Page 314 of the *Encyclopaedia Britannica* kept in Ernest Shackleton's cabin during the Imperial Trans-Antarctic *Endurance* Expedition, 1914–17. © National Maritime Museum, Greenwich, United Kingdom

pressing than the provision of mental nutrition. This included the lighting of fires and pipes, rolling seaweed or sennegrass cigarettes, and serving as toilet paper. Among the handful of surviving pages, brought back to England by surgeon Alexander Macklin, are numbers 314 to 332, focusing on embryology, and representing the contemporary debates over how penguin embryology could potentially contribute to understanding evolutionary biology.

32

BANJO

After the loss of the *Endurance* during the Imperial Trans-Antarctic Expedition of 1914–17, Ernest Shackleton instructed his men to keep just 900g (2lb) of personal gear. Worried about the creeping boredom and despair that can be fatal in polar expeditions, an exception was made for this 5.4kg (11.9lb) zither banjo, 'the last thing to be saved off the ship before she sank', according to Shackleton, 'and I took it with us as a mental tonic'.

The instrument belonged to meteorologist Leonard Hussey, who was selected to join the expedition despite having no experience with meteorology. According to one shipmate: 'The vagaries of the climate quite bewilder Hussey. For just when he thinks it is going to do one thing the precise opposite happens.' However, if he was a poor meteorologist, Hussey was invaluable in keeping up the good spirits of the team and 'with his cheeriness and his banjo, was another vital factor in chasing away any tendency to down-heartedness'.

In Antarctica, one of the greatest threats comes from oppressive boredom, especially in the long polar winter. Following the loss of *Endurance*, keeping up morale became especially vital for survival, and Hussey's talents took on greater weight than in other circumstances. The often-complaining Thomas Orde-Lees even praised Hussey fulsomely: 'He is a banjoist of unusual merit and it is very pleasant to have music of any kind down here; his repertoire is sufficient to prevent his tunes becoming too monotonous.' Indeed, even while waiting for rescue on Elephant

Island, Orde-Lees noted that the 'banjo ... really does, as Sir Ernest said, supply brain food; not exactly intellectual food, but music hath charms altogether unique on Elephant island'.

The men were not the only ones to appreciate Hussey's music. Shackleton recounted an anecdote from December 1914: 'During the afternoon three adelie penguins approached the ship across the floe while Hussey was discoursing sweet music on the banjo. The solemn-looking little birds appeared to appreciate "It's a Long Way to Tipperary," but they fled in horror when Hussey treated them to a little of the music that comes from Scotland.'

Nearly every account of the expedition makes several references to the relief that Hussey's banjo brought them. Popular songs played by Hussey included 'Swanee River', 'Little Brown Jug' and 'John Peel'. Symbolising the instrument's importance in keeping the men united, the banjo was later signed by several members of the expedition.

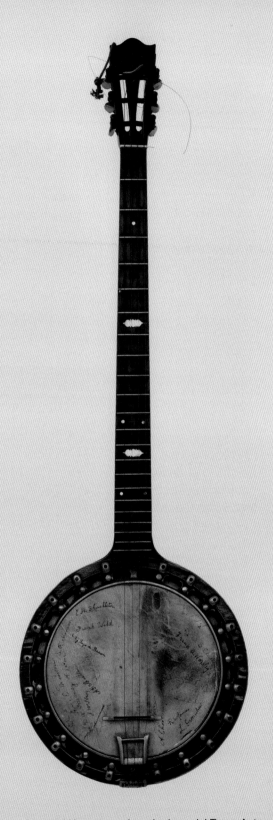

Banjo belonging to Leonard Hussey used on the Imperial Trans-Antarctic *Endurance*
Expedition, 1914–17. © National Maritime Museum, Greenwich, United Kingdom

33

JAMES CAIRD

When the *Endurance* sailed from England for Antarctica in 1914, she carried three lifeboats, each named for a major donor to the Imperial Trans-Antarctic Expedition: *James Caird*, *Dudley Docker* and (Janet) *Stancomb Wills*. When *Endurance* sank on 21 November 1915, crushed by sea ice in the Weddell Sea, these three lifeboats became the men's best hope for survival.

It was on board these boats that in early April 1916 the expeditioners made for the islands off the Antarctic Peninsula and landed on Elephant Island on 15 April. While safer than the floating ice, Elephant Island was still very hostile. The seal and penguin population was migratory and could not be relied upon for food. The island was not well sheltered and so the men could easily freeze or be swept out to sea. It was so isolated that they would be unlikely to be found by passing whaling or sealing ships. Their most realistic chance was for some of them to seek rescue from one of the whaling stations on the island of South Georgia, over 1,200km (745 miles) north-east.

Speed was essential. On 20 April, Shackleton announced his plan to take five men and sail towards South Georgia. Much depended on Henry McNish, the ship's carpenter, who used the party's spare resources to make the *James Caird* more seaworthy. Before leaving the sea ice, he had already cannibalised timber from the *Endurance* to raise the sides of the *Caird* by 25cm (10in), fashioning a makeshift caulk from seal blood, oil paint and lamp wicks. Once on Elephant Island, he reinforced the hull with the mast of the *Stancomb Wills* and improvised a deck covering with sledge runners and a stretch of canvas. On 24 April, the *James Caird* was launched. Frank Wild, who had been left in command on the island, had the two remaining boats turned into makeshift shelters.

The *James Caird*'s trajectory was through some of the most treacherous waters on Earth. The crew of six were assigned to four-hour watches, during which three men would attempt to sleep in what navigator Frank Worsley called 'indescribably

uncomfortable' circumstances. Two would pump out water while the sixth took the helm. Fixing position was incredibly challenging as the sun was rarely visible and the sea was constantly pitching the boat. Able seamen John Vincent and Tim McCarthy would hold Worsley around the waist. Worsley pointed his sextant at the sun, with Shackleton crouching below with the chronometer. At night, Worsley steered by stars and, in no visibility, he simply estimated the direction. Ending what is often referred to as one of the greatest boat journeys ever undertaken, the *James Caird* finally landed on the southern shores of South Georgia on 10 May.

Knowing that the whaling stations were on South Georgia's northern shores, Shackleton set out to cross the island with Crean and Worsley. The trio hiked for 36 hours straight. On 20 May, they finally reached Stromness.

Shackleton now focused his efforts on rescuing the remaining men from Elephant Island. After several attempts to secure a ship capable of making the journey, Shackleton finally persuaded the Chilean Navy for use of the Coast Guard vessel *Yelcho*. The small vessel reached Elephant Island on 30 August 1917, 128 days after Shackleton departed. All the men were rescued.

Launching of the *James Caird* on 24 April 1916 during the Imperial Trans-Antarctic *Endurance* Expedition, 1914–17. Photo by Frank Hurley. © Getty Images/Royal Geographical Society

34

MEMORIAL CROSS

While Shackleton is often lauded for losing no men despite the loss of the *Endurance,* this oft-repeated praise misrepresents reality. It is true that no men died on board his ship, but the 1914–17 Imperial Trans-Antarctic Expedition included two parties: Shackleton's own crossing party, and the Ross Sea Party. The latter consisted of a group of ten men, instructed to lay food depots between the Ross Sea and the South Pole to support Shackleton's intended crossing.

After establishing a base at Scott's *Terra Nova* base at Cape Evans, their ship, the *Aurora*, was torn from its moorings and went adrift, stranding the party. Overcoming many difficulties, the men managed to sledge hundreds of miles, laying depots that would ultimately never be used.

It was on one of these long sledging journeys that the Ross Sea Party experienced its first fatality. Chaplain and photographer Arnold Spencer-Smith, suffering from scurvy as well as exhaustion, died on 9 March 1916. The team was distressed by his loss, and physicist Richard W Richards later recalled that 'All through the long weeks of his journey on the sledge we had tried to do what we could to lighten his lot   Now, within two days march of comparative safety, his loss seemed indeed tragic.' The men buried Spencer-Smith in the ice and erected a snow cairn over his grave with a makeshift cross on top.

On their way back from laying depots, the men took shelter at Hut Point, built during the 1901–04 *Discovery* expedition. By early May, exasperated with the unvarying diet of seal meat and nervous that they might miss a rescue ship, expedition commander Aeneas Mackintosh and general assistant Victor Hayward announced their intention to walk back to their base at Cape Evans, despite the onset of winter and unsafe ice conditions. Their companions objected but Mackintosh and Hayward set off nonetheless and were never seen again. After the return of the sun, the remaining party members conducted a thorough, though fruitless search. Before departing the continent, they erected a cross at Wind Vane Hill, Cape Evans, to stand in remembrance of fallen members of the Ross Sea Party.

The risk of death was omnipresent for early Antarctic explorers. Of the 664 men who took part in Antarctic expeditions between 1895 and 1922, 19 died of causes varying from nutritional deficiencies and starvation to drowning and falling into crevasses. Between 1922 and 1961, during a period that saw an enormous growth of people working in Antarctica, 30 men were lost by the United States alone. These deaths exclude the countless numbers of whalers and sealers who died in the region. Deception Island and South Georgia both have graveyards dedicated to men lost at sea or otherwise killed during the hunts. Ernest Shackleton himself died and was buried on the island of South Georgia, where his grave has become a pilgrimage site.

While the death rate in Antarctica is now very low, tragedy still strikes and human losses are still memorialised, reminding all visitors to beware and treat Antarctic environments with respect. If Antarctica is fragile, so are humans.

Memorial cross dedicated to Aeneas Mackintosh, Arnold Spencer-Smith and Victor Hayward on Wind Vane Hill, Cape Evans, Ross Island. © Jean de Pomereu

35

RADIO TRANSMITTER

Antarctic exploration is often compared to the exploration of space. Among the many differences, however, is that space exploration has always benefited from radio contact with mission control, whereas long-distance communication was slow to emerge in Antarctica. During the Heroic Age of Antarctic exploration, Douglas Mawson's 1911–14 Australasian Antarctic Expedition and Ernest Shackleton's 1911–14 Imperial Trans-Antarctic Expedition both attempted to use wireless radio communication, but various mishaps resulted in failure.

Starting in the 1920s, American science and technology came to dominate Antarctic exploration and it was the American 'hero' of the Antarctic, Richard Byrd, who first succeeded in using radio technology while on the continent. Byrd's Antarctic expeditions began an era when journeying towards the South Pole no longer meant disconnecting with human civilisation.

'Halo; wing of the Fokker Airplane crashed on March 12 1934.' By David Paige. © Byrd Polar and Climate Research Center Archival Program, The Ohio State University, Columbus, United States

Byrd's first Antarctic expedition, 1928–30, involved two ships, *City of New York* and *Eleanor Bolling*, and three aeroplanes: a Ford Trimotor (*Floyd Bennett*), a Fairchild FC-2W2 (*Stars and Stripes*) and a Fokker Super Universal (*Virginia*). As a way to garner publicity for his expedition, Byrd held a nationwide competition searching for an exemplary Boy Scout to join his expedition. He selected Paul Siple, who served on all five of Byrd's following expeditions and was later the lead scientist at the United States' South Pole station during the 1957–58 International Geophysical Year.

Upon arrival on the Ross Ice Shelf, Byrd and his men constructed a base camp at Little America and began a series of scientific and geographical investigations. On 28 November 1929, Byrd, pilot Bernt Balchen, co-pilot/radioman Harold June and photographer Ashley McKinley flew the *Floyd Bennett* to the South Pole and back in 18 hours 41 minutes. They had difficulty gaining altitude and had to dump empty gas tanks and their emergency supplies out of the plane door to achieve the altitude of the Antarctic Plateau. One thing they did not throw overboard was a radio-transmitter, identical to the one pictured here, which allowed them to stay in touch with Little America for the duration of their flight.

Transmitter, Heintz and Kaufman, Type B1, Richard Byrd's Antarctic expedition, 1928–30. Photo by Benjamin G Sullivan. © Courtesy of the Smithsonian National Air and Space Museum, Washington DC, United States

This particular transmitter belonged to the Fokker Super Universal, which in March of 1929, was caught in a blizzard and torn from its moorings. The radio was destroyed, leaving the three men stranded without means of communication until they were rescued several days later. The transmitter was eventually recovered from the plane's wreckage in 1934, during Byrd's second Antarctic expedition, as memorialised by artist David Paige.

Byrd's first Antarctic expedition is considered to be the dawning of the Mechanical Age of Antarctic exploration. It was during Byrd's second expedition, however, that the first successful radio broadcast was made from Antarctica and transmitted to household radio sets in the United States, bringing Antarctica right into people's living rooms. Indeed, with radio transmitters and aeroplanes alike, Antarctic exploration would never be the same.

36

POST OFFICE SAFE

While the United States' government has never made a formal territorial claim in Antarctica, in the 1930s it was not entirely clear that they never would. Evidence of this possibility can clearly be seen in relation to Little America's Post Office safe.

In order to commemorate Robert Byrd's second Antarctic expedition of 1933–35, the United States Post Office Department issued a postage stamp designed by Franklin Roosevelt, a collector himself. It was the first to be designed by a sitting president. The 3-cent Byrd Antarctic Expedition commemorative stamp was issued on 9 October 1933. It was intended solely for philatelic use on

mail sent to Little America. A 50-cent surcharge was added to the price of the stamp to offset the cost of transportation.

The Post Office Department also sent postal clerk Charles F Anderson on Byrd's expedition to cancel mail for philatelic collectors at Little America, located at the Bay of Whales on Antarctica's Ross Ice Shelf. Arriving in Antarctica in November 1934, Anderson found that numerous letters sent the previous year had not been processed. Working in conditions just warm enough to keep the ink from freezing, he prepared a total of 153,217 mail pieces in just 16 days. This combination lock safe stored stamps, cancellation dies and other valuables at the small temporary postal station. The Little America Post Office was closed in 1935.

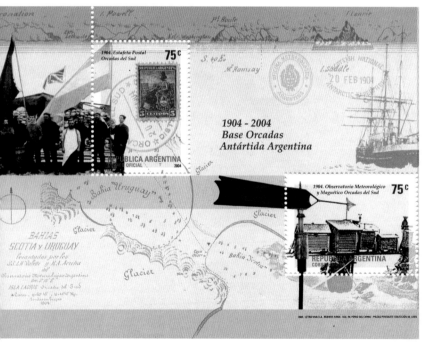

Souvenir sheet commemorating the 100th anniversary of the South Orcadas Magnetic and Meteorological Observatory and the creation of the South Orcadas Post Office in Argentine Antarctica. © Correo Oficial de la República Argentina S.A.

More recently, the Post Office at the United Kingdom's Port Lockroy on the Antarctic Peninsula, renovated in 1996 as a museum primarily for cruise ship passengers, boasts its status as the southernmost post office in the world. It is operated by the United Kingdom Antarctic Heritage Trust and posts over 70,000 letters each year to more than 100 countries.

Post offices, particularly in an imperial context, have served as a symbolic means of territorial authority, reinforced by the confidence of their users. Postal stamps too are often created to symbolically enforce territorial claims. Antarctica's liminal status, in regard to sovereignty, spawned the creation of post offices in both permanent and temporary bases, but also a proliferation of postal stamps, especially from countries with territorial claims such as the United Kingdom, France, Australia and Argentina, which has the longest established post office, Base Orcadas, opened in 1904. The preponderance of polar stamps has resulted in the creation of various societies around the world dedicated to polar philately. But beyond the fun of stamp collecting or mailing a letter from Antarctica dwells the past – and present – of imperialism and sovereignty disputes in Antarctica.

Little America Post Office safe. © Smithsonian Institution
National Postal Museum, Washington DC, United States

37

PEMMICAN

With few local sources, a major concern for Antarctic visitors is obtaining and ingesting nutritious food. During the Heroic Age of Antarctic exploration, the lack of fresh food sources led to many health problems for expeditioners, most notably scurvy and malnutrition. In the words of Australian explorer Douglas Mawson, 'good and suitable food reduces to a minimum the danger of scurvy; a scourge which has marred many polar enterprises'. Men typically relied on canned meats, canned and dried vegetables, canned fruit, cereals, flour and tea. This was supplemented with fresh seal meat, fish and even penguins. Desserts were saved for special occasions.

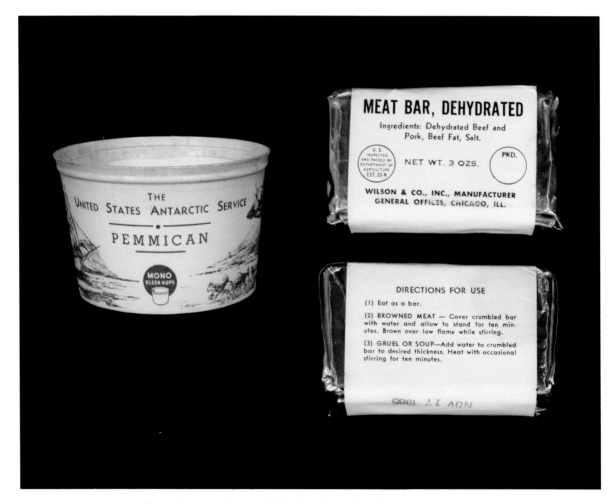

Pemmican container and dehydrated meat bar. Photo by Mystie Do.
© Museum of Texas Tech University, Lubbock, United States

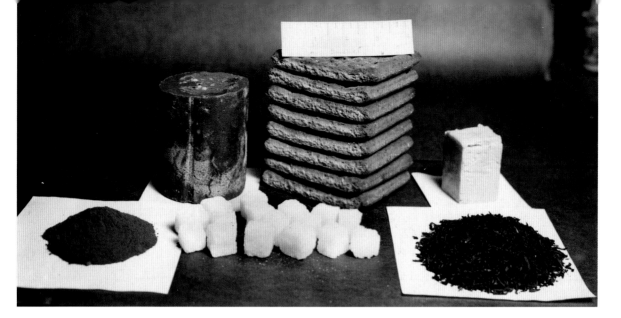

Pemmican, hardtack, butter, cocoa, sugar and tea. Sledging rations for one man for one day, Antarctica, 1912, British Antarctic *Terra Nova* expedition 1910–13. Photo by Herbert Ponting. © Getty Images/Royal Geographical Society

Beyond health problems, the monotonous diet of early explorers meant that the men were often obsessed with food. Members of the *Endurance* expedition, which relied almost entirely on seal meat near the end, often passed the time by describing their ideal meals or favourite foods, with one man even rescuing a cookbook from the ship. Richard Byrd, who spent his five months alone in Antarctica in 1934, wrote in his memoir of the experience of a time when 'I found the cook book! … The whoop of joy I uttered sounded so loud that I was actually embarrassed. … No book washed ashore to a castaway could have been more avidly studied.'

Even when men were in less dire circumstances, they were relieved when special occasions like Christmas or Midwinter's Day resulted in celebratory dinners, complete with niceties uncommon in other circumstances. The tradition of celebrating special occasions with festive foods continues at many research stations to this day, even though a wider variety of foods is more readily available and regularly resupplied during austral summer months. For example, on New Year's Eve, visitors to the United States' McMurdo Station have been known to enjoy Beef Wellington and fresh lobster flown in from New Zealand.

The issues with food in Antarctica are more pronounced when people journey inland. Food is heavy and fieldwork is extremely labour intensive. Compounded with the extreme cold, an average adult who may normally only need 2,000 calories in a day could need up to four times that if engaged in particularly demanding work such as man-hauling a sledge. Additionally, any food must be easily preparable while in the field. Hardtack, the name given to long-lasting plain wholemeal biscuits, was another sledging essential. Pemmican, a mixture of dried meat, cereal and melted fat, first developed by Indigenous people of North America, was also adopted by polar explorers as a high-energy food. Pemmican and hardtack were sometimes mixed with water to make 'hoosh', a filling stew that unfortunately lacked the vitamins to stave off scurvy.

Both on base and in the field, people still prioritise food high in carbs and protein. Since the Heroic Age, chocolate bars and powders have been a staple of field expeditions as they are lightweight, high in calories and tasty. Even today, some long-distance travellers in Antarctica will eat entire sticks of butter, trying to consume enough calories to survive. Without drastically increasing your food intake, living and working in Antarctica can be deadly.

38

POLAR STAR

By the early 1930s, the South Pole had been reached by Roald Amundsen and Robert Falcon Scott, and flown over by Richard Byrd. Despite Shackleton's efforts with the *Endurance*, crossing Antarctica remained the next big prize in the continent's exploration, with flight considered the most viable method.

The son of a Chicago coal magnate, Lincoln Ellsworth had already funded and participated in Roald Amundsen's failed attempt to fly to the North Pole in 1925, as well as in the Norwegian's successful attempt in 1926. Anxious to inscribe his own name in the annals of exploration, Ellsworth next set his sights on crossing Antarctica. He persuaded Hubert Wilkins, a pioneer of Antarctic aerial exploration in the late 1920s, to serve as his adviser, and commissioned a specially built two-seat ski-equipped Northrop Gamma, which could fly at 350km/h (217.5mph), land on ice, and be strapped down in case of storms in the

Landing site and camp during Lincoln Ellsworth and Herbert Hollick-Kenyon's flight across Antarctica, 23 November 1935. © Smithsonian National Air & Space Museum, Washington DC, United States

field. It was also large enough to carry a sledge, skis, tents, sleeping bags, stoves and necessary provisions in case they lost the plane.

After two failed attempts at crossing the continent, Ellsworth invited Herbert Hollick-Kenyon, a Canadian First World War veteran experienced in flying Arctic rescue missions, to come on board as his pilot. The *Polar Star* took off from Dundee Island at the northern tip of the peninsula on 23 November 1935. The destination was Little America, an abandoned station first established by Richard Byrd in 1928. Little America was located 3,800km (2,361 miles) away on the coastline of the Ross Sea. Reaching it required flying over thousands of kilometres of unexplored territory. In Ellsworth's own words: 'We were the first intruding mortals in this age-old region, and looking down on the mighty peaks, I thought of eternity and man's insignificance.'

Ellsworth and Hollick-Kenyon encountered several dangerous setbacks during their journey. After 14 hours, they made the first of four landings, crumbling the fuselage of their aircraft and destroying their radio. Despite this, they managed to take off again the next day, but a storm forced them to land once again and take shelter for three days. Weather conditions forced them to land two more times before they ran out of fuel and made their final landing, 40km (25 miles) short of Little America, on 5 December 1935.

Lincoln Ellsworth's 1933 Northrop Gamma *Polar Star*. This was the first plane to fly across Antarctica, 23 November to 5 December 1935. Photo by Eric Long. © Smithsonian National Air & Space Museum, Washington DC, United States

The flight they had expected to make in 14 hours had taken 14 days, with 20 hours spent in the air. They had discovered two mountain ranges and claimed 900,000sq km (347,492sq miles) of Antarctic territory on behalf of the United States (which the United States government never formally acknowledged). Ellsworth and Hollick-Kenyon completed their first crossing of Antarctica on foot, reaching Little America on 15 December. There, they had to wait a month before eventually being rescued by the British research vessel *Discovery II*.

39

SOAP

While whalers were present in the Antarctic throughout the 19th century, systematic and large-scale hunts in the region can be dated to the early 20th century, when British-Norwegian whaler Carl A Larsen applied for British whaling leases for his new company, Compañía Argentina de Pesca. This lease was granted in 1906 by the governor of the Falkland Islands and Dependencies, William Allardyce, who touted the region as 'the Whaler's El Dorado'. Larsen also began the construction of Grytviken, on the island of South Georgia, which became a centre for Southern Ocean whaling. This first whaling venture paid a 70 per cent dividend in the first year, a number so impressive that by 1911, eight whaling companies operated seven stations in South Georgia.

For the next 50 years, whales were hunted extensively throughout the Southern Ocean. Whale oil was a valuable commodity. It was an ingredient in explosives that were used in the First World War, as well as margarine in the face of a global shortage of fats. It was also an important source of industrial lubricants and used in the production of soaps, cosmetics and fertilisers. According to British biologist Stanley Kemp, the Southern Ocean whale field 'proved more productive than all those in the rest of the world combined'. In the context of this whaling boom, Great Britain made its first Antarctic territorial claim in 1908.

Pressured by scientists who were concerned about the effect of such wide-scale and sometimes wasteful harvesting, Great Britain's Colonial Office organised the Discovery Committee, which, beginning in 1924, conducted investigations to provide the scientific background to stock management of the commercial Antarctic fishery. While largely a veneer for British commercial interests, the *Discovery* investigations resulted in 37 major reports on whale migration, diet and behaviour.

When, in the 1940s, Argentina and Chile began to dispute British territorial claims in the region.

Britain used its management of the Southern Ocean whale fishery as a basis for its claim to sovereignty. With this, 'Great Britain alone undertook the responsibilities of sovereignty and performed the functions of a state'.

Whales were thus not just economic resources to be extracted as raw material, but geopolitical tools for which management could form the basis of territorial claims.

A whale on the flensing plan at Grytviken, South Georgia. Photo by Frank Hurley, 1917. © Getty Images/Scott Polar Research Institute, University of Cambridge, United Kingdom

Sapoceti Guerlain 'Savon au Blanc de Baleine' whale oil soap, Paris, 1950s.
© South Georgia Museum, South Georgia

40

SWASTIKA STAKE

In 1938–39, Germany undertook its third Antarctic expedition, by order of Hermann Göring. Led by polar explorer Alfred Ritscher, the Deutsche Antarktische Expedition's main objective was to establish a whaling station and acquire fishing grounds to reduce Germany's dependence on foreign imports. In January 1939, the MS *Schwabenland* reached Queen Maud Land, located within Norway's Antarctic territorial claim. There, its members used two seaplanes to survey and map approximately 350,000sq km (350,000sq miles), discovering previously unknown ice-free mountains and lakes. At the turning points of the flights, 1.2m (3.9ft)-long aluminium stakes embossed with swastikas were dropped to establish German claims to ownership of the territory, which Ritscher dubbed New Swabia. None of these arrows have ever been recovered.

Example of stakes dropped from aircraft to claim territory during the German Antarctic Expedition of 1938–39. Published in Alfred Ritscher's 1942 *Wissenschaftliche und fliegerische Ergebnisse der Deutschen Antarktischen Expedition 1938–39.*

Upon the *Schwabenland*'s return to Hamburg in April 1939, Germany issued a decree about the establishment of a German Antarctic sector. Despite this, it never officially advanced a territorial claim for the region and no lasting German structure was built until the construction of the Neumayer Station as a research facility in Queen Maud Land in 1981.

Perhaps because of a combination of the secrecy over the original expedition, the charismatic combination of both Nazis and Antarctica, and for many years the scant public information over its progress, this expedition became fodder for conspiracy theorists. In 1947, Hungarian exile Ladislas Szabo published *Hitler est vivant*, in which he claimed that a submarine convoy had carried members of the Nazi leadership to Antarctica at the end of the Second World War, where they settled in a base called New Berchtesgaden.

Others have since argued that from a base allegedly established by Ritscher's men in 1939, Nazi scientists were at work creating advanced military technology, which manifested as UFOs hostile to enemy aircraft. One version of this story suggests that the 1946–47 United States Navy Antarctic Developments Program, known as Operation *Highjump*, ended early due to specific fears over enemy planes, possibly Nazi-constructed UFOs. Although these myths have been widely debunked, other writers have since seized and elaborated upon these stories, which continue to circulate the internet.

The idea of Antarctic Nazis is not the only conspiracy theory surrounding Antarctica. Flat Earth theorists, rather than considering Antarctica to be one of seven continents, usually depict it as an ice wall that surrounds a disc-shaped Earth. The Hollow Earth Theory, widely popularised in the 19th century, suggests that the Earth is a hollow shell with openings at each pole. Inside the Earth is a lush subterranean world, inhabited by anything from aliens to mythological geographies like Atlantis or the Garden of Eden. In fact, in another version of the mythology surrounding Operation *Highjump*, US naval forces were repelled from the region by UFOs emerging from the Hollow Earth. Some have even claimed that Byrd himself flew into the Earth during his 1926 North Pole flight.

Despite Antarctica's global designation as a continent for science, its mysteries and allure, as well as the fact that most people will never have the opportunity to go there, have meant that it has also been designated as a region ripe for conspiracy theories. Some, like the idea of Antarctic Nazis, are rooted in history.

Members of the German Antarctic Expedition holding a Nazi flag in Antarctica. Photo by Siegfried Sauter. Published in Alfred Ritscher's 1939 *Die Deutsche Antarktische Expedition 1938–39*. Vorbericht über die Deutsche Antarktische Expedition 1938–39.

Logo of the German Antarctic Expedition 1938–39. Cover of Alfred Ritscher's 1939 *Die Deutsche Antarktische Expedition 1938–39* Vorbericht über die Deutsche Antarktische Expedition 1938–39.

41

MITTENS

It was in 1946, during the Ronne Antarctic Research Expedition, that the first women travelled to Antarctica and wintered there as members of a geographical expedition. The Ronne Expedition, organised by American polar explorer Finn Ronne, whose father had been a member of Roald Amundsen's *Fram* expedition, was the last privately sponsored American Antarctic expedition. Based on Stonington Island, it explored and mapped the Weddell Sea coast, the last uncharted coastline in the Antarctic.

Photograph of Finn Ronne and Edith 'Jackie' Ronne in Antarctica, 1947. © Courtesy of the Ronne family

Although it is commonplace for women today to be members of Antarctic expeditions, their ability to participate has often been riddled with institutional and cultural challenges. In the first half of the 20th century, it was not unusual for women to be present on the subantarctic island of South Georgia or even on whaling ships. In fact, the earliest human remains discovered in the Antarctic belonged to an Indigenous woman from southern Chile, buried in the early 1820s on the South Shetland Islands, having presumably travelled south on board on a whaling or sealing vessel.

The Ronne Antarctic Research Expedition was not originally meant to include women. After departing from Texas, Edith 'Jackie' Ronne, the commander's wife, and Jennie Darlington, the wife of the expedition's pilot, had intended to leave the ship in Panama. The decision to stay on board meant that on reaching Stonington Island, Jackie Ronne had only a suit, a dress, nylon stockings and high heels to wear. She and Darlington had to be fitted with men's gear.

In Antarctica, Jackie Ronne took over her husband's intended role as the expedition's recorder, compiling daily activities so she could write short news articles and press releases on the expedition for the North American Newspaper Alliance. Her writings formed the basis of Finn Ronne's book *Antarctic Conquest*, published in 1949, which he dedicated 'to my wife Edith, who was an anchor to windward and saw the whole expedition through me'. Jackie Ronne was also a general assistant for some of the scientific research activities. In her leisure time, she and Darlington contributed to the upkeep of the station and, like the men, engaged in familiar relaxing activities such as reading and knitting. Darlington is notable for being one of the first, if not the first, woman to become pregnant

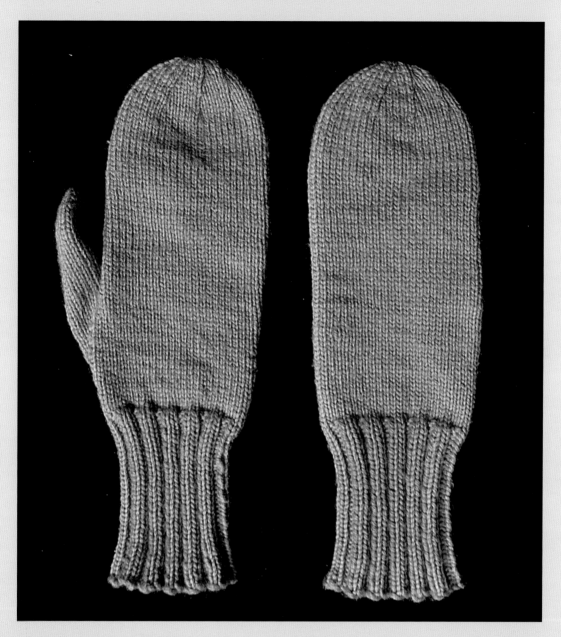

Mittens knitted in the Antarctic by Edith 'Jackie' Ronne during the Ronne Antarctic Research Expedition, 1946–48.
© Courtesy of the United States Navy History and Heritage Command, Washington DC, United States

in Antarctica, which she revealed to the other expedition members by eating an entire jar of pickles in one sitting.

Darlington and Ronne both published memoirs about their experiences but took very different perspectives on their time. While Darlington concluded that 'women do not belong in Antarctica', Jackie Ronne was not only the namesake of Edith Ronne Land (now the Ronne Ice Shelf), but she also returned to Antarctica 15 times and was a fellow of the Explorers Club and president of the Society of Women Geographers. Jackie Ronne died in 2009.

42

SUIT

The Antarctic Peninsula is contested territory. Claimed by Argentina, Chile and the United Kingdom, the long geopolitical dispute over this region has manifested in many different ways, both physical and symbolic.

Chile made its first territorial claim to the Antarctic Peninsula in 1940. This followed the United Kingdom's claim in 1908 and preceded an Argentine claim in 1942. Starting in 1943, the three countries began constructing meteorological stations throughout the peninsula. Argentina, which had maintained a meteorological research station on the South Orkney Islands since 1904, occupied the region for the longest continuous period. In 1946, Juan Perón, of Argentina, prefaced a pamphlet on Antarctic sovereignty by criticising those nations that attempted to occupy and claim territory that he regarded as rightfully belonging to Argentina.

Besides these three conflicting claims, the proliferation of Antarctic activity from the United States – which did not acknowledge any of the existing claims – provoked worry in the political, military and scientific communities of Chile, Argentina and the United Kingdom. Starting

in the 1940s, the United Kingdom and Argentina began engaging in gunboat diplomacy, sending naval vessels into the region, taking down each other's flags and flying their own instead.

Chilean president Gabriel González Videla also rallied public support for Chilean activity in

Gabriel González Videla giving a speech in Antarctica, 1948. © Colección fotográfica, Museo Histórico Presidente Gabriel González Videla. La Sirena, Chile, Servicio Nacional del Patrimonio Cultural. Ministerio de las Culturas, Las Artes y el Patrimonio

the region, emphasising the possible military and economic advantages. Chile based its sovereignty claim on two primary factors. First, it emphasised the historical ties between Spanish and Chilean explorers who had made claims to the southern Atlantic. Second, it highlighted their shared physical and environmental geography whereby the Antarctic Peninsula is a natural continuation of its national Andean territory.

In a 1947 speech to the Senate of Chile, Minister of Foreign Affairs Raúl Juliet Gómez announced that Chile would shortly organise an expedition and 'For scientific purposes and in order to carry out a more effective expression of our sovereignty over Chilean Antarctica, a meteorological and magnetic base will be established on this trip ... As proof of our sovereignty, the expedition will leave in different places in the Antarctic territory, marks and signs that proclaim the rights of Chile. This is a practice that has been put into use since the first polar explorations, and we have found it convenient to adopt, since it makes known to foreign eyes the effectiveness of the occupation and the scope that its sovereignty encompasses.'

Contributing to the symbolic geopolitical gestures, Gabriel González Videla became the first head of state to visit Antarctica when he and Chile's first lady Rosa Markmann Reijer sailed with the Chilean Navy in February 1948 to take possession personally of Graham Land and the other Antarctic territories claimed by Chile.

Videla also inaugurated a second Chilean station, the Base General Bernardo O'Higgins Riquelme, named for the father of Chilean independence. Today, Chile maintains 13 research bases, all located within the territory it originally claimed in 1940.

'Thermal suit' used by Chilean president Gabriel González Videla on his trip to Antarctica in 1948.
© Colección fotográfica, Museo Histórico Presidente Gabriel González Videla. La Sirena, Chile, Servicio Nacional del Patrimonio Cultural. Ministerio de las Culturas, Las Artes y el Patrimonio

43

SLEDGE WHEEL

The further one ventures into Antarctica's interior and across its great ice sheet, the more the topography starts to resemble that of the open sea. The horizon is unbroken for 360 degrees and the only surface features are the parallel wave-like *sastrugi* formed by the wind and drift.

As well as coping with the cognitive monotony of travelling across such barren regions, the biggest challenge for explorers is the absence of any vegetational, geological or human features to establish notions of scale, distance and perspective. Sometimes described as a negative geography, the surface of the Antarctic ice sheet challenges our ability to position ourselves in space and time.

In order to navigate across such regions before the advent of GPS, early explorers used a combination of dead reckoning, chronometers, compasses and sextant readings to set a course and to determine their location and plot their progress on a map. Chronometers and compasses were used to set bearings or to check a course and dead reckoning allowed quicker travel between readings. A simple way to set a rough bearing was to use shadows – a technique still employed today. Snow cairns were sometimes also built to help expeditions find their way on their return journey.

Also key to navigation, positioning and surveying were sledge wheels (or sledge metres). First developed by American and European explorers in the Arctic – for example, during the exploration

Sledge wheel used by the Norwegian-British-Swedish Antarctic Expedition, 1949–52. © Scott Polar Research Institute, University of Cambridge, United Kingdom

and mapping of the Greenland ice sheet in the later decades of the 19th century – these devices most often consisted of simple bicycle wheels, attached to the back of a sledge via a pole ending in a fork containing the wheel. They were equipped with odometers that mechanically counted the number of rotations of the wheel as it was pulled behind the sledge, thus establishing the distance travelled. While odometers could vary in design and became more precise with time, sledge metres operated in the same way whether the sledges were pulled by men, dogs, ponies or mechanised vehicles.

The sledge wheel shown here was used during the Norwegian-British-Swedish Antarctic Expedition, 1949–52. Although most expeditions before this point were composed of members from more than one country, the NBSX was the first Antarctic expedition to be organised jointly by different nations. It was thus the first truly

Explorers pull a sledge packed with supplies across snow and ice during the British Antarctic *Terra Nova* expedition, 1910–13. © Getty Images/Hulton Deutsch

international Antarctic expedition and a starting point for the international collaborative spirit that still underpins much Antarctic research today. As a truly modern post-war expedition, the NSBX had at its disposal a number of tracked, fuel-powered Weasels to provide transport. When it came to the exploration and mapping of Antarctica's interior, however, it relied on a team of about 40 dogs to pull the sledges fitted with sledge wheels.

As purely mechanical devices, sledge wheels are sometimes still used today as a form of back-up by expeditions weary of electronic instruments and their sometimes unreliable performance in extreme conditions.

44

HAORI

This kimono-style jacket (*haori*) celebrates the establishment of the Showa Station, located on East Ongul Island in Queen Maud Land, built for Japan's Antarctic contribution to the International Geophysical Year of 1957–58.

The origins of the International Geophysical Year (IGY) are well documented. On 5 April 1950, American physicist James Van Allen invited a group of scientists to a dinner in honour of the British geophysicist Sydney Chapman. After dinner, their conversation shifted to the state of the field of geophysical sciences. The Second World War had led to the development of many new inventions that could be used for co-ordinated, international observations across the globe, and would lead to greater scientific knowledge in the oceans, poles, atmosphere and space. Based on this, American physicist Lloyd Berkner suggested a renewal of the two previous International Polar Years of 1882–83 and 1932–33.

By the summer of 1950, Berkner and Chapman had made a formal proposal to the Mixed Commission on the Ionosphere. The commission then drew up a resolution in support of a Third International Polar Year and presented it to the International Council of Scientific Unions (ICSU), a non-governmental federation of 13 international scientific unions. The ICSU immediately formed a special committee for the organisation of such an event, but many of the unions were concerned about its focus on the Polar Regions. Chapman then proposed the name 'International Geophysical Year'.

While 67 countries eventually participated in the IGY, only 12 were active in the Antarctic. These 12 states later became the original signatories

Taiichi Kitamura feeds Taro and Jiro, the two surviving dogs, at Showa Station on 14 January 1959, at the start of Japan's third Antarctic expedition. © The Asahi Shimbun/ Getty Images

of the Antarctic Treaty: Argentina, Australia, Belgium, Chile, France, Japan, New Zealand, Norway, South Africa, the United Kingdom, the United States and the Soviet Union. The IGY was not only a huge endeavour for the scientific community but was fervently covered by the press and sparked the public imagination.

Made in 1957–58, this *haori* depicts penguins in a frozen landscape, gazing at an ice-breaker ship. This ship was the *Sōya*, originally an ice-strengthened cargo freighter. *Sōya* was requisitioned by the Imperial Navy during the Second World War, when she participated in the 1942 Battle of Midway. In 1950, the ship received a comprehensive refit in preparation for service as Japan's first dedicated Antarctic research ship.

In 1958, the *Sōya* made international news when, at the end of the IGY, she provided an emergency evacuation for the men at Showa. However, with winter closing in, poor weather conditions prevented the helicopter from airlifting their dogs. Of the 15 dogs left behind, Taro and Jiro survived the winter and were discovered by the next research group the following spring. Several monuments were constructed to honour the fortitude of these two animals.

Japan's Showa Station remains one of the most important research facilities on the Antarctic continent, one of four stations under the auspices of the Japanese Antarctic Research Expedition (JARE). Since its establishment in 1956, JARE has been responsible for many major projects, including meteorological recordings, ecosystem studies and deep ice-coring.

45

TRACTOR

In 1953, British geologist Vivian Fuchs began to circulate a proposal for what he named the Commonwealth Trans-Antarctic Expedition (TAE). Fuchs stressed both the romantic origins and the scientific potential of his plan, which he asserted took initial shape as he sheltered from a blizzard while working for the Falkland Islands Dependencies Survey, but there were also geopolitical motivations to his proposal.

Edmund Hillary's tractor 'Sue', during the Commonwealth Trans-Antarctic Expedition 1955–58. © Antarctica New Zealand Pictorial Collection

At the time, the United Kingdom's claims in Antarctica were under increasing threat from Argentina and Chile. Even the American Expedition to the Weddell Sea in 1947–48 did not acknowledge British sovereignty. In Fuchs' words, 'A trans-continental journey made wholly within territory claimed by the British Commonwealth ... would gain prestige and at the same time contribute to the solidarity of Commonwealth interests.'

Once plans for the International Geophysical Year (IGY) of 1957–58 had been announced, Fuchs tied the TAE to the scientific programme of the IGY. Even though the TAE would remain separate, it could be seen as supporting the IGY's wide-ranging scientific research efforts. Fuchs soon won the support of many in the polar and scientific communities across the Commonwealth. To succeed in journeying from the Weddell Sea to the Ross Sea via the South Pole, Fuchs' plan, much like that of Ernest Shackleton's attempt to cross the continent 40 years earlier, depended on a supporting party from New Zealand. Led by Edmund Hillary, an international celebrity since his 1953 ascent of Mount Everest, this party would lay depots of food and fuel to support Fuchs' journey from the South Pole to the Ross Sea.

Hillary began his food and fuel depot-laying journey from New Zealand's newly established Scott Base in the Ross Sea region on 14 October 1957. In order to save costs and reflect New Zealand's agricultural strengths, Hillary travelled with three Massey Ferguson TE20 tractors, modified with a full tracking system for use in the snowy conditions. Hillary and his team made good time in

these vehicles and established Depot 700, their last scheduled depot, in late December.

In the meantime, Fuchs' team had encountered rough conditions and crossed the continent much more slowly than expected. Seeing an opportunity, Hillary continued to the South Pole and reached the United States' South Pole station on 3 January 1958, thus becoming the first to do so using overland vehicles. By the time Fuchs arrived at the pole on 20 January, a media firestorm had exploded, characterising the expedition as a 'race to the pole' by two national parties, rather than as a single unified Commonwealth expedition. Like the first race to the pole between Roald Amundsen and Robert Falcon Scott, and to the great annoyance of Fuchs, this was presented as another race lost by the United Kingdom. Fuchs' crossing party returned to Scott Base on 2 March 1958, completing its historic 3,473km (2,158 mile) return journey.

Between 1992 and 2015, an image of a modified Massey Ferguson tractor graced the New Zealand $5 note, in commemoration of Hillary's achievement.

Edmund Hillary on a New Zealand $5 note, 1999–2015.

46

STATUE

Bleached by the circling sun, facing north in the direction of Moscow, the plastic bust of Lenin at the Antarctic Pole of Inaccessibility (POI) is one of the strangest sights in Antarctica.

At the height of the Cold War, after the United States declared its plans to build a station at the Geographic South Pole (90° South) within the context of the International Geophysical Year (IGY), the Soviet Union settled on a double consolation prize consisting of the Geomagnetic Pole and the POI. Located at the furthest point from any coastline within the centre of Antarctica, and as one of the coldest places on Earth, the POI (average temperature -58.2°C (-72.8°F), altitude 3,724m (12,218ft) was a significantly more hostile location than 90° South. As such, it matched Soviet ambitions in demonstrating that Russian explorers could operate in much harsher environments than those occupied by the Americans. It also meant that the Soviets could concentrate their IGY efforts in East Antarctica, while the Americans focused on West Antarctica and the Ross Sea region.

A party of 18 men from the Third Soviet Antarctic Expedition first reached the POI on 14 December 1958. Led by scientist Yevgeny Tolstikov, the group traversed 2,110km (1,311 miles) from the Soviet Union's new coastal station, Mirny, on board powerful tracked vehicles pulling sledge-mounted living containers. Once in situ, they established a 24sq m (258sq ft) hut equipped with an electric furnace, a radio shack and a generator. During a short ceremony that included the firing of rockets and the raising of the Soviet flag, the men erected a bust of Lenin on the chimney rising high from the station roof.

This kind of nationalist marking of territory was common in Antarctica at the time and persists today.

Over the next 12 days, the Soviet party carried out seismic, gravitational, magnetic and meteorological observations. On 18 December, a Lisunov Li-2 twin engine landed next to the hut and flew four men back to Mirny. By 26 December, despite having enough provisions for six months, it was decided that the station was too remote for permanent use and the remaining men headed back north towards the coast.

The POI has only been revisited a handful of times since. The first was in 1964 by the Ninth Soviet Antarctic Expedition, and the second in 1965 by the United States Antarctic Research Expedition. Recently, however, it has become a goal for adventure tourism and one of the most exclusive 'selfie' locations on Earth. Using foil kites, the British N2i team were the first sporting adventurers to reach it in 2007. Photographer Sebastian Copeland followed in their footsteps in 2011. By then, most of the station had sunk into the snow and only the top of the chimney and Lenin still emerged from the surface, keeping watch on the frozen wastes.

Bust of Lenin at the Pole of Inaccessibility, erected by the Third Soviet Antarctic Expedition in 1958. Photographed by Sebastian Copeland during his Antarctica Legacy Crossing, 2011. © Sebastian Copeland

47

DYNAMITE

Despite the perception of Antarctica as a silent realm, dynamite detonations have been a persistent component of the continent's soundscape since the start of the 20th century.

Among the first times the explosive was used on the Antarctic continent was in digging a grave for zoologist Nicolai Hanson, a member of Carsten Borchgrevink's 1898–1900 *Southern Cross* expedition who perished in 1899 after a long decline. Located at the top of a hill overlooking the expedition's wintering hut at Cape Adare, Hanson's grave is still visible today.

Seismologist Lizzy Clyne prepares explosives to place into a shot-hole near the grounding zone of Thwaites Glacier, 2020. © Kiya Riverman

An equally dramatic use for explosives in Antarctica was during desperate attempts to free ships imprisoned in the pack ice. The first such incident took place in 1899 when the crew of Adrien de Gerlache's *Belgica* used tonite to help create a channel through which their vessel finally escaped after a long and unplanned year beset in the ice. Dynamite was used during Robert Falcon Scott's 1901–04 *Discovery* expedition, Erich von Drygalski's 1901–03 *Gauss* expedition, and Jean-Baptiste Charcot's first Antarctic expedition, 1903–05, on board the *Français*. Although use of the explosive freed the *Discovery,* it was not powerful enough to free the *Français* or the *Gauss*. The *Français* was eventually freed thanks to saws and pickaxes, but the *Gauss* remained stuck until the ice broke up around her naturally a year later. Ernest Shackleton, on the other hand, failed to include dynamite among the supplies of the 1914–17 *Endurance* expedition, possibly contributing to the ship's loss.

Another important use of dynamite in Antarctica is for seismic sounding, a technique used to measure the depth of land ice and map the bedrock beneath it. Developed by Swiss scientists to measure the depth of Alpine glaciers in the inter-war period, and then used to probe the Greenland ice sheet during Alfred Wegener's 1930–31 German Greenland Expedition, seismic sounding was first used in Antarctica during an inland traverse carried out by the 1949–52 Norwegian-British-Swedish Antarctic Expedition. The technique consisted of detonating dynamite

Seismic sounding explosion using dynamite to measure the depth of land ice during the International Geophysical Year, 1958–59. © Estate of Graham Knuckey

on the surface of an ice mass to create sound waves. Then, with the use of a very sensitive device known as a seismograph, scientists measured how long the waves took to travel down through the ice and back up again, having rebounded on the bedrock beneath. Taking into account the velocity of ice, it was then possible to calculate the thickness of the ice mass at this particular location. In the words of Ernst Sorge, one of the early pioneers of seismic sounding, 'our instruments, like X-rays, enabled us to "see" through the ice of the underlying ground'.

By repeating soundings at regular intervals along a traverse trajectory, scientists were then able to draw up a profile or cross section of ice masses and, eventually, to determine their volume and evaluate how much a particular ice body might contribute to sea level rise if it melted. Dynamite continues to be an essential tool in Antarctic science and exploration, not only for seismic sounding, but also for exposing crevasses, collecting marine samples and searching for dinosaur fossils.

48

KHARKOVCHANKA

Of all the motor vehicles that have been tested in Antarctica, the Soviet-designed *Kharkovchankas* are among the most remarkable. Not only did they transport heavy loads and passengers across the continent, but they also contained 28sq m (301sq ft) of tight but comfortable living and working accommodation for up to eight men. Using a Soviet heavy artillery tractor chassis as their base, the first three *Kharkovchankas* were designed and manufactured in just three months at the state-owned Malyshev Factory in Ukraine.

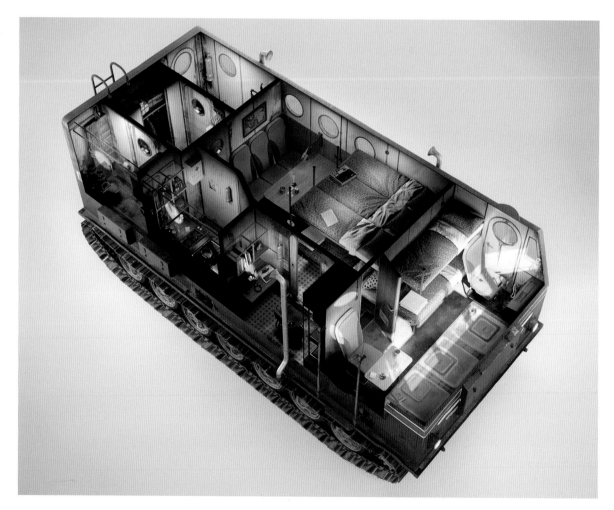

Illustration of interior of a *Kharkovchanka*, comprising driver cabin, living quarters, communication centre, galley and bathroom. © Engage Studios, Moscow, Russia

Weighing 35 tons and measuring 8.5m (27.9ft) long, 3.5m (11.5ft) wide and 4m (13.1ft) tall, the *Kharkovchankas* were completely self-contained, allowing engineers to work on the engine and scientists to carry out their research from the sheltered interior. The accommodation included eight berths, a bathroom and toilet, a galley, a mess table, a navigation compartment, a workshop and a vestibule. The *Kharkovchankas* were insulated with eight layers of wool and had heating systems embedded in the windows to keep them ice-free. Rarely driven faster than 10km/h (6.2mph) their huge weight meant they burned more than 10 litres of fuel per kilometre (3.5 gallons per mile). Even with this high level of consumption, they could still manage up to 1,500km (932 miles) without refuelling.

Two *Kharkovchankas* were delivered to Antarctica in 1959, towards the end of the International Geophysical Year. Shortly thereafter, the *Kharkovchankas* undertook an 89-day, 5,4000km (3,355 miles) return journey from the coastal Mirny Station to Vostok Station and on to the Geographic South Pole, where they surprised United States' personnel living at the newly established South Pole station. They were greeted with open arms and stayed at the pole for three days, during which the American and Soviet flags flew side by side.

Improved versions of the *Kharkovchanka* continued to be utilised well into the 2000s and some remain on the continent today as historic monuments. While *Kharkovchankas* were the first habitable Antarctic vehicles to prove successful in the field, the idea for such machines originated with the Antarctic Snow Cruiser, a 17m (55.8ft)-long 6m (19.7ft)-wide behemoth that moved on huge rubber wheels rather than tracks. Developed for the 1939–41

United States Service Expedition, the Cruiser provided accommodation for five men and was also designed to carry a five-seat Beechcraft biplane on its roof.

Manufactured in Chicago by the Armour Institute of Technology at a cost of $300,000 USD (more than $5 million USD today), the Cruiser proved a public sensation. Its troubled history, however, started when it slid off a small bridge on its way to the port of Boston and was trapped in a river for three days. Delivered to Antarctica in January 1940, its smooth tyres proved incapable of gaining traction on the snow.

The Snow Cruiser being loaded onto a ship bound for Antarctica as part of Richard Byrd's 1939–41 expedition. © Byrd Polar and Climate Research Center Archival Program, The Ohio State University, Columbus, United States

Fortunately, engineers soon found it could move backwards and so the Cruiser completed a number of short scientific journeys. Eventually abandoned in the vicinity of Little America Station, it was buried by snowfall and re-excavated twice, in 1946 and again in 1958. It was then engulfed by snow once more and has by now probably floated off the Ross Ice Shelf within an iceberg, and dropped to the bottom of the ocean.

49

CREVASSE DETECTOR

In the words of the American geophysicist John C Cook, 'crevasses are natural deathtraps'; one of the most lethal features of the Antarctic landscape. This is especially the case when they are covered and made invisible by snow bridges resulting from accumulation and drift.

During the 1911–14 Australasian Antarctic Expedition, Belgrave Edward Sutton Ninnis and his dog team fell to their deaths in a hidden crevasse. In 1956, during Operation *Deep Freeze*, US naval serviceman Max Kiel died driving a D8 tractor that fell into a crevasse.

In 1965, Jeremy Bailey, David Wild and John Wilson, who had been in the cab of a Muskeg near the United Kingdom's Halley research station, were swallowed by a crevasse. Bailey, though 'all smashed up', survived the initial fall, but died in his attempt to climb out.

Crevasse detector used during the traverse of the Ross Ice Shelf during Operation *Deep Freeze*, 1957–58. Photo by William Cromie. © William J. Cromie Images, Byrd Polar and Climate Research Center Archival Program, The Ohio State University, Columbus, United States

One answer to such omnipresent dangers was the introduction of crevasse detectors such as the one shown here. Projecting about 4.8m (15.7ft) from the lead vehicle, they used electrodes to find electrical anomalies indicative of cracks in the ice. They were utilised by the United States' Filchner Ice Shelf Traverse during the 1957–58 International Geophysical Year. But even with this new technique, explorers still relied on the older method of sending a man ahead, anchored with a rope, to probe the snow's surface using a long steel rod. Neither practice was foolproof and vehicles still sometimes broke through the thin snow bridge.

According to American naval officer and artist Standish Backus, 'On any glacial ice, but more especially on any part of the Antarctic continental glacier, a traveller lives constantly under the Damoclean threat that a crevasse may be under him. Without warning, the snow that has bridged over the yawning maw, rendering it indistinguishable, may give way. Men and machines may be instantly swallowed down forever, down perhaps hundreds of feet of undulating, ice-blur depths.'

Despite the ongoing development of new technologies such as thermal infrared sensors and battery-powered robots able to carry a ground-penetrating radar, crevasses remain a clear and present danger in Antarctica. In separate incidents in 2016, American climate scientist Gordon Hamilton and Canadian pilot David Wood both died after falling into crevasses. Crevasses are also responsible for copious injuries, loss of equipment and time delays when travelling across the ice.

Crevasses serve as a reminder that as much as humans gain relative safety and experience in the Antarctic, hidden dangers remain with every footstep taken further into the ice. Indeed, in the words of American seismologist John Bernhardt, 'safety in crevasses is a relative term'.

50

TREATY

The International Geophysical Year (IGY) of 1957–58 resulted in a significant increase in international interest in the Antarctic. While only four countries had permanent research stations in Antarctica prior to the IGY, that number grew to 12 by 1958. Although most often attributed to peaceful scientific collaboration, this expansion was also driven by geopolitical interests.

Exacerbated by the successful launch of *Sputnik* in 1957, the Cold War meant that tensions between the United States and the Soviet Union could potentially spill over into Antarctica. Moreover, the years leading to the IGY had already seen an increase in tensions between Argentina, Chile and the United Kingdom, three of the seven claimant states. In 1952, shots were fired in Hope Bay on the Antarctic Peninsula in an incident between Argentina and the United Kingdom. In 1955, the United Kingdom filed cases against Argentina and Chile with the International Court of Justice over their respective territorial claims in the region.

These tensions, coupled with fears that the Soviet Union might act to expand its grasp on the region, prompted the convening of an Antarctic Conference to agree on a framework for the future governance of the continent. Representatives from the 12 nations active in Antarctica during the IGY met in Washington DC over an 18-month period. Their negotiations resulted in the drafting and signing of the Antarctic Treaty on 1 December 1959, with its implementation coming into force in June 1961.

The treaty designates Antarctica as a continent dedicated to peace and science, bans military manoeuvres and promotes the continuation of free scientific investigation and co-operation. Moreover, Article V of the treaty bans nuclear

explosions and the disposal of radioactive waste on the continent, making it the first non-nuclear proliferation treaty of the Cold War. The controversial Article IV, however, maintains a certain status quo in stating that the treaty is explicitly not 'a renunciation by any Contracting Party of previously asserted rights of or claims to territorial sovereignty in Antarctica'.

The Antarctic Treaty has vastly expanded since 1961, evolving into the Antarctic Treaty System with the adoption of many subsequent agreements, mostly concerned with environmental protectionism. These agreements include: Agreed Measures for the Conservation of Antarctic Fauna and Flora (1964), the Convention for the Conservation of Antarctic Seals (1972), the Convention for the Conservation of Antarctic Marine Living Resources (1982) and the Protocol on Environmental Protection to the Antarctic Treaty (1991), which bans all forms of mineral exploitation. The long-standing success of the Antarctic Treaty System has also inspired a slew of other scientific and environmental treaties, including the 1967 Outer Space Treaty.

Despite its successes, however, the Antarctic Treaty System also has its vulnerabilities and limitations. For example, the geographical boundaries of the treaty allowed the Anglo-Argentine conflict in 1982, over the Falkland

Islands/Las Islas Malvinas to spill onto the subantarctic island of South Georgia. Moreover, the seven claimant countries still only build bases in their claimed territory, thus tacitly insisting on their regional sovereignty should the treaty falter in the future.

Antarctic Treaty, 1959. © Courtesy of the National Archives of Australia, Parkes, Australia (NAA:A6180, 1/8/75/22)

First meeting of Antarctic Treaty countries after treaty signing, July 1961, By National Publicity Studios, Wellington. © Antarctica New Zealand Pictorial Collection, 1961

51

DOG FUR BOOTS

At the height of the Cold War, geopolitical and scientific tensions between the United States and the Soviet Union seemed as fraught as they might ever be. While the International Geophysical Year (IGY) of 1957–58 and the launch of *Sputnik* initiated the Space Race, the IGY also paved the way for exchanges of Soviet and American scientists in Antarctic research stations in an effort at mutual peace and co-operation through science.

In 1960, American glaciologist Gilbert Dewart was stationed with a Soviet research team during the Fifth Soviet Antarctic Expedition, both at the Mirny Station and during a four-month summertime trek to the Vostok Station, located inland near the Southern Pole of Inaccessibility, the furthest point from any coastline. At the same time, Russian geophysicist Leonid Kuperov was invited to winter at the United States' McMurdo Station to study radio field intensities. Within six weeks, however, he was evacuated for medical treatment in New Zealand.

On arrival at Mirny, Dewart was issued three types of boots: high, leather military boots; *valenki*, thick felt boots traditionally worn by Russian peasants; and a pair of dog fur boots described as warm, thick, fur and leather boots. Dewart wrote that he 'liked the convenience of the high pull-on boots and preferred them to the fussily laced American footwear'. While excellent for cold and dry weather, these boots were less useful in the summer melt season due to the thawing conditions and the accompanying risk of trench foot. In addition to his dog fur boots, Dewart was also issued a sleeping bag with an outer lining 'coarsely made out of dog pelts'. While fur clothing was common in earlier expeditions, by the 1960s, a period of transition, much fur-based gear had been replaced by synthetic materials. This surviving pair of boots

Cover of Mikhail Artem'evich Kuznetsov's *Under the roofs of Mirny*, Izdatel'stvo Transport, Moscow, 1964. © Courtesy of the Scott Polar Research Institute, University of Cambridge, United Kingdom

Pair of dog fur boots,
C Stewart Gillmor
Collection of Soviet
Polar Clothing. ©
Peary-MacMillan Arctic
Museum, Bowdoin
College, Brunswick,
United States

was issued to C Stewart Gillmor, an American ionospherist who replaced Dewart at Mirny as part of the Sixth Soviet Antarctic Expedition.

Besides contributing to the scientific programme at Mirny, Dewart saw this as an opportunity to work out 'a cultural export program of my own that I hoped would give my Russian hosts a sample ... of American literature and popular music'. In Dewart's memoir, *Antarctic Comrades*, he relates a generally positive experience at Mirny, where the team, consisting not only of Soviet but also of Czech and German scientists, bonded over geophysical research, heavy drinking, good food and watching films.

In fact, Dewart 'was more often struck by the similarities between Russians and Americans than by the differences'.

Although geopolitical relations between the United States and the Soviet Union continued to deteriorate during his year at Mirny, Dewart recalled a pledge of support from a Soviet seismologist who said 'let none of this affect our relationship with our good comrade Gil. Whatever problems may exist between our governments, let our personal friendship live on.' Dewart even asserted that 'Antarctica seemed to be the only place in the world where Russians and Americans were still on speaking terms'.

52

FUEL DRUMS

Nothing has sped up the pace of Antarctic exploration more than the introduction of the combustion engine and the burning of fossil fuel. Indeed, extreme environmental conditions and the absence of any easily exploitable local energy sources has meant that dependence on fossil fuels has been greater in Antarctica than on perhaps any other continent.

Barrels filled with fuel at the South Pole, 1957. Photo by Cliff Dickey. © National Science Foundation.
Courtesy of United States Antarctic Program Photo Library, United States

While seal and whale oil were once exported from the Antarctic to power lights and street lamps, the first fossil fuel to be imported to Antarctica was the coal used to power ships, cook and keep warm. At dawn of the 20th century came petrol, kerosene and acetylene gas. Acetylene was employed for lighting wintering huts and kerosene was used in Primus stoves. Petrol, on the other hand, was used to power the first experimental wheeled and tracked vehicles brought to Antarctica.

It was only with the introduction of aircraft and more sophisticated tracked vehicles from the 1920s onwards that Antarctic exploration's ongoing dependence on fossil fuels really began. This was accentuated by the increasing use of fuel to heat and power research stations, and the fact that transporting just one drum of oil on the continent could require the burning of two or more extra drums. The result was an exponential growth in the number of fuel drums that were dispensed to Antarctica each year, many of them gifted by oil companies such as Exxon and British Petroleum.

The most paradoxical aspect of fossil fuel consumption in the Antarctic, however, was that the exploration of some of the most susceptible environments to global warming was made possible by the very practice that caused the warming in the first place. A particularly visible impact was the empty drums that rapidly accumulated around research stations and in the field, and which were regularly left behind when camps and stations were abandoned. In the worst cases, this resulted in drums slowly deteriorating and residual fuel spilling into the environment. This negligence, combined with the accumulation of other kinds of Antarctic waste, eventually grabbed the attention of environmental organisations in the 1980s and resulted in numerous clean-up operations by national Antarctic programmes and NGOs such as the 2041 Foundation.

Today, while drums still play an important role in fuel distribution, most of the fuel consumed in Antarctica is stored in much larger permanent tanks and fuel is more often transported in large bladders, pulled across the snow surface by tracked vehicles. Most promising, however, is the transition to renewable energy that is currently underway as national Antarctic programmes have come to realise the savings that can be made by building wind turbines and harnessing the solar energy that pours onto the continent during the summer months.

Among the successes of this ongoing transition is Belgium's Princess Elisabeth Station, Antarctica's first zero-emission station, and the Venturi Antarctica, designed in Monaco the first zero-emissions tracked exploration vehicle on the continent.

Belgium's Princess Elisabeth Station, built in 2007, which is able to operate solely on solar and wind power during the summer months. © International Polar Foundation, Brussels, Belgium

53

PROJECTION REELS

In Antarctica as elsewhere, one of the most popular forms of entertainment is watching films. This is especially the case during the long winter months, when sharing suspense and laughter acts as a social bond.

Before the first film projectors made it to Antarctica, sharing stories took the form of group readings, or putting on skits and plays, which often included cross-dressing. Lantern-slide lectures also provided a more studious escape from the frozen desolation of Antarctica.

Post-war, film projection reels were transported to Antarctica, and once there were rarely sent back. This resulted in bountiful film libraries at stations across the continent. Among the largest of these film libraries was the one at the Soviet Bellingshausen Station on King George Island, where a large room was dedicated to storing hundreds of projection reels. While these films were subject to approval by the Soviet Communist Party, the collections found at other stations comprised all genres. The collection at France's Dumont d'Urville station, for example, reflected France's penchant for auteur films and was screened in a projection room that doubled up as the smoking room.

With the shift to video, an ever widening selection of films, series and documentaries became available to Antarctic personnel. The projection reels that had accumulated over the years became redundant vestiges of a bygone era. A vast majority of the films that could be found in Antarctic video libraries were set far from the continent, with selections most often reflecting national tastes. Increasingly, however, they also included films and documentaries that focused on the Antarctic.

Some of these were shot in Antarctica to document specific expeditions, research programmes and natural phenomena, for example, Frank Hurley's 1999 *South*, Luc Jacquet's 2005 *March of the Penguins* and Werner Herzog's 2007 *Encounters at the End of the World*. The majority, however, were filmed in studios and mountain ranges thousands of miles from Antarctic shores.

Beginning with the 1948 classic *Scott of the Antarctic*, starring John Mills and filmed in London and Norway, these films comprised of many period dramatisations of major historic

expeditions. These include *The Last Place on Earth*, a 1985 miniseries recounting Amundsen and Scott's race to the South Pole; *Shackleton*, a 2002 miniseries about the *Endurance* expedition; and the 1983 *Antarctica*, with music by Vangelis, recounting the peculiar tale of the 15 dogs abandoned by the Japanese expedition of 1957–58.

Among the very rare fiction films that were at least partly shot in Antarctica was the 1971 commercial flop *Mr Forbush and the Penguins*, as well as the 2019 *Where'd You Go Bernadette*, whose critical reception was not much better. As for fictional films set in Antarctica, but not filmed there, the most commercially successful was the 2006 animation *Happy Feet*.

The most iconic, however remains John Carpenter's 1982 *The Thing*, a horror movie in which Antarctic scientists encounter a parasitic extraterrestrial creature that assimilates, then imitates other organisms. *The Thing* has achieved cult status, especially with station

Man and camera at the South Pole, 1957. Photo by Cliff Dickey. © National Science Foundation. Courtesy of United States Antarctic Program Photo Library, United States

personnel, who like to scare themselves by watching it again and again during the darkest months of the Antarctic winter – when escape is not an option.

Film projection reels from France's Dumont d'Urville research station. © Courtesy of the French Polar Institute and the Cinémathèque de Bretagne

54

RADIO ECHO SOUNDER

In 1971, watching a screen in the hold of a United States Navy Hercules aircraft flying over East Antarctica, British electronics engineer Michael Gorman could see entire mountain ranges while the crew on the flight deck witnessed nothing but featureless ice and snow stretching in all directions. The instrument that allowed Gorman to peer through the ice surface and visualise the hidden mountainous topography beneath was a Mark IV radio echo sounder – a type of radar.

In contrast to seismic sounding, which required detonating dynamite on the surface of an ice mass, radio echo sounding (RES) devices emitted radio waves on a continuous basis and recorded in real time their rebound from the bedrock beneath the ice. Resembling submarine sonars, RES systems could also be operated from moving vehicles, thus greatly speeding up the surveying process while also obtaining much greater precision than the seismic method.

The discovery that radio waves could be used for subglacial mapping is owed at least in part to human tragedy. As an increasing number of aircraft were deployed to the Antarctic after the Second World War, it became apparent that the radar altimeters used by pilots to determine their altitude failed to register the ice surface, as the waves they emitted penetrated straight through. When combined with poor visibility, this resulted in a succession of planes crashing into the ice, killing a reported 19 men during United States Operation *Deep Freeze* missions of 1955–61. It was in analysing the data from these crashes that Amory 'Bud' Waite, a radio engineer at the United States Army Signal Corps, grew aware that radio waves could be adapted to map the topography of bedrock beneath the ice.

First tested on board tracked vehicles travelling over the Greenland ice sheet, airborne radio echo sounders were eventually deployed in Antarctica on board helicopters in the early 1960s. As a result of a collaboration between the United States Antarctic Program, which provided the aircraft and logistics, and the Scott Polar Research Institute and Technical University of Denmark, which engineered and operated the RES devices, the late 1960s and 1970s saw the deployment of RES systems in aircraft such as the United States Navy Super-Constellation and Hercules. These systems included antennas fixed beneath the wings and fuselage of the aircraft. Not only could they visualise the bedrock topography, the devices were also sensitive enough to detect the internal layers of snow and ice that make up an ice sheet.

In addition to collecting close to 180,000km (111,850 miles) of profiles that provided a basis for mapping parts of the Antarctic ice sheet in three dimensions, the RES campaigns confirmed with greater precision the existence of features first identified by earlier seismic sounding techniques. Among them were Lake Vostok and the Gamburtsev mountain range, two features first suggested by Soviet seismic sounding campaigns during the 1957–58 International Geophysical Year, which have since proved crucial to our understanding of Antarctica's geological and glacial history.

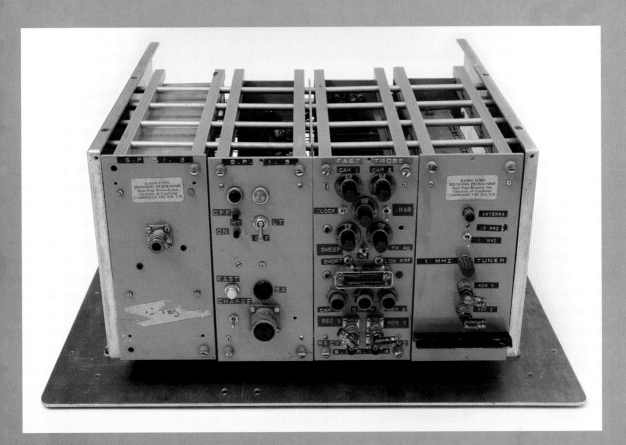

Mark IV radio echo sounding device, set on anti-vibration mounting, manufactured by the Scott Polar Research Institute, 1969. © Scott Polar Research Institute, University of Cambridge, United Kingdom

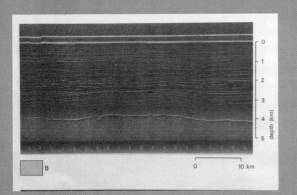

Radio echo sounding profile from the Scott Polar Research Instititute's *Antarctica: Glaciological and Geophysical Folio*, 1983. © Scott Polar Research Institute, University of Cambridge, United Kingdom

55

FROZEN BEARD

A quintessentially masculine image associated with the Antarctic is the ice-encrusted beard of the rugged polar explorer. During the Heroic Age, these beards were practical. Since water was in short supply, shaving was an unnecessary luxury. When outdoors, however, the moisture from the men's breath or the water from their eyes streamed downwards and froze. During the *Endurance* expedition, Ernest Shackleton commented: 'The beards even of the younger men might have been those of patriarchs, for the frost and the salt spray had made them white ... Our beards and moustaches are masses of ice.'

Frozen beards could be painful. The ice stuck to facial covering and when this clothing was pulled away, it took hair with it. Carrying so much ice on their faces also made men far more prone to frostbite. Although regular shaving became more practical over time, it remained popular for Antarctic personnel to grow beards, despite their disadvantages. Indeed, far from clean-shaven civilisation, beards were also regarded as an emblem of frontier spirit and masculinity.

Beard-growing competitions were also quite popular in Antarctica. American military artist Standish Backus, who painted some of these specimens, later commented: 'Facial Hirsuteness, whether a product of expediency or glory, has always been an accepted mode for well-dressed polar inhabitants. Many members of the Operation *Deep Freeze* entered the hairy sweepstakes whole-heartedly with their whole chins. Winners of local honors frequently were as surprised at what happened when they stopped shaving as the losers were dismayed by what refused to grow.'

The tradition of the frozen Antarctic beard endures today. In 2008, the Natural History Museum in London organised an advertising campaign around the visage of the frozen beard, showing several images of young boys in outdoor gear, frozen beards superimposed on their faces. In 2013, an overwinterer at Australia's Mawson Station wrote, as he listed 25 different facial hair styles: 'With a contingent of 15 red blooded males, facial hair, along with that on our heads has been allowed to live life freely ... In other words, should you wish to let yourself go, Antarctica is the place.'

The Champ. By Standish Backus, 1956. © Courtesy of the United States Navy History and Heritage Command, Washington DC, United States

The close association between a frozen beard and Antarctica reminds us that even today, when we envision a stereotypical polar explorer, it is a person who can grow a beard.

James C Peteison, at the end of eight months of isolation at the South Pole station in 1961. © United States Navy, National Science Foundation. Courtesy of the United States Antarctic Program Photo Library, United States

56

NUCLEAR REACTOR

Signed in the middle of the Cold War, the Antarctic Treaty stipulated that nuclear explosions and the disposal of radioactive waste are prohibited in Antarctica. While this clause prevents Antarctica from becoming a site for testing and deploying nuclear weapons, it does not prohibit the peaceful use of nuclear energy at research stations, in the field or on board ships.

Examples of this peaceful use of nuclear energy include the 45 Radioisotope Thermoelectric Generators (RTGs) that powered automatic weather stations and other data collection efforts in Antarctica between 1961 and 2015. Fuelled with small amounts of strontium 95, these compact devices are much simpler in design than nuclear reactors and could power a simple weather station in the remotest locations on the continent for ten years or more, transmitting data to satellites every few minutes or even seconds. Many of these devices were deployed by American and French scientists, sometimes

The main panel board of the nuclear power plant at McMurdo Station, 1963. © United States Navy, National Science Foundation, Courtesy of the United States Antarctic Program Photo Library, United States

semi-secretly via nuclear-free countries such as New Zealand and Australia. The greatest number, however, were operated by the Soviet Union, and later Russia. Despite their excellent safety record, RTGs have now been withdrawn from Antarctica through a co-ordinated international effort.

By far the most significant peaceful nuclear device in Antarctic history, however, was the PM-3A portable nuclear reactor shipped to Antarctica and installed at the United States' McMurdo Station amid much fanfare in 1962. Fuelled with highly enriched uranium, able to produce 1.8 megawatts of electricity, and operated by a team of 25 men from the Naval Nuclear Power Unit, PM-3A was meant to dramatically reduce the United States Antarctic Program's consumption of fuel. Right from the start, however, it was plagued with problems, including fissures in the reactor, corrosion of the cooling circuit, and the release of radioactive water into the surrounding environment. A total of 448 malfunctions were recorded and led to the reactor being nicknamed 'Nukey Poo'.

Since the United States and its senior leadership had publicly hailed the reactor as the embodiment of 'a dramatic new era in man's conquest of the remotest continent', its problems were hushed and patched up until they became so serious that 'Nukey Poo' had to be shut down in 1972. The dismantling of the reactor started the following year, and because the Antarctic Treaty stipulates that all nuclear waste must be removed from the continent, the Navy removed more than 12,000 tons of contaminated soil from under the facility and shipped it to the United States for disposal.

Completed in 1979, this process was carried out without protective gear by United States Navy personnel and a handful of New Zealand Army cargo handlers. Some of these men and others who worked at McMurdo Station at the time have since developed particularly aggressive cancers and blamed 'Nukey Poo'. Reports have been filed in New Zealand and legal actions have been taken in the United States, but compensations and the recognition of mishandling by military and governmental institutions have become entangled in legal quagmires.

The location of 'Nukey Poo' was later designated as a Historic Site, but all that remains is a carved-out hillside and a plaque.

PM-3A portable nuclear reactor, 'Nukey Poo', being installed at McMurdo Station, 1962. © Navy Nuclear Power Unit, United States Seabee Museum, Port Hueneme, United States

57

DOG CARDS

Personnel files usually include a good deal of information regarding employees, their skills, major behavioural incidents, and their noteworthy achievements. The same can be said for the files kept by the British Antarctic Survey (BAS) about their dogs.

The BAS dog card system was set up in 1952 to control and monitor their breeding programme. Each card in this filing case contained key information. It started with the dog's name, number, sex and date of birth, along with pertinent information about its parentage. It also included either a photograph of a particular dog or a generic drawing of a canine marked with an individual's major physical characteristics. Recorded on the front of the card was its positive and negative character traits, which praised attributes like 'hardworking', 'fast' or 'intelligent', while condemning traits like 'timid' and 'high strung'. The front also included its medical history, while the back recorded its work achievements, its position in the team, and its participation in specific long journeys. Finally, it recorded the dog's progeny.

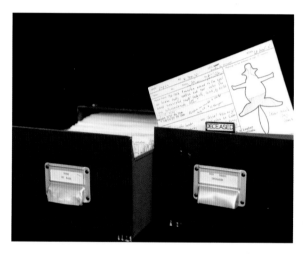

Dog card box. © British Antarctic Survey Archives Service, Cambridge, United Kingdom (ref. AD8/2)

The 1898–1900 *Southern Cross* expedition, which relied on expertise from Sami dog drivers, was the first to use dogs in Antarctica. Dogs went on to become vital to the success of science and exploration on the continent until the 1990s. Not only did they pull sledges over large tracts of snow, allowing for relatively reliable travel, they also served a psychological purpose as expeditioners formed intense bonds with individuals and their teams.

Yet sledge dogs were working animals, not pets. As such, they often met gruesome ends in Antarctica, falling through crevasses, drowning,

or even being killed by other dogs. Because they could not be safely converted into family pets, they often needed to be put down when no longer able to work. This created public relations issues in the wake of the 1955–58 Commonwealth Trans-Antarctic Expedition, when New Zealand schools sponsored the purchase of sledge dogs for the expedition. Children remained invested in and named the dogs, making their eventual disposal a tricky issue.

While extremely important to Antarctic exploration, sledge dogs were not environmentally neutral. They mostly lived on seal meat, hunted from the local marine mammal population. They would also, given the opportunity, kill waterbirds.

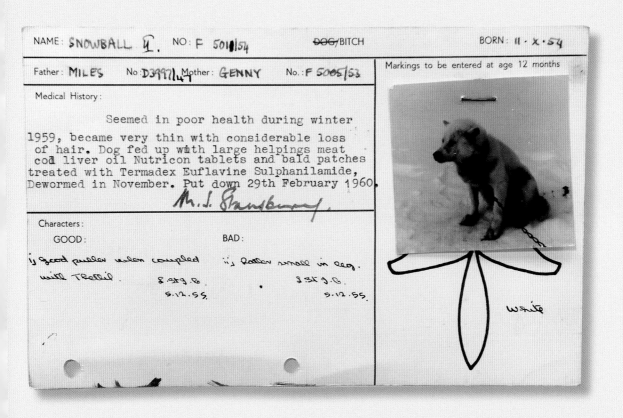

NAME: SNOWBALL ♀. NO: F 501/54 ~~DOG~~/BITCH BORN: 11·x·54

Father: MILES No: D3997/44 Mother: GENNY No: F 5005/53

Markings to be entered at age 12 months

Medical History:

    Seemed in poor health during winter
1959, became very thin with considerable loss
of hair. Dog fed up with large helpings meat
cod liver oil Nutricon tablets and bald patches
treated with Termadex Euflavine Sulphanilamide,
Dewormed in November. Put down 29th February 1960.

       M.J. Stansbury.

Characters:
 GOOD: BAD:

is good puller when coupled is rather small in leg.
with Trellis. 8.9 9.6.   23 9.6.
    5.12.55.   5.12.55.

white

Dog card for 'Snowball,' progeny of 'Miles' and 'Genny'. © British Antarctic Survey Archives Service, Cambridge, United Kingdom

With the introduction of mechanised transport through the 1960s and 1970s, dog sledges became less useful. In 1991, the environmental protocol of the Antarctic Treaty, attempting to curb invasive species in the region, indicated that 'Dogs shall not be introduced onto land, ice shelves or sea ice'. The last dogs, a team of 14, were removed from BAS' Rothera Base in 1993 and transported to Canada.

In 2009, a bronze sculpture of a sledge dog, created by British artist David Cemmick, was unveiled in front of BAS headquarters in Cambridge. This statue, presented by former BAS employees, memorialised the 1,204 dogs that worked for BAS between 1945 and 1993. Today, this memorial stands in front of the Scott Polar Research Institute at the University of Cambridge, reminding visitors that not all Antarctic explorers were human.

58

MS *LINDBLAD EXPLORER*

While a very small handful of fee-paying passengers travelled to the South Shetland and Orkney islands on board support vessels from as early as the 1920s, it was only in 1969 that Lars-Eric Lindblad, a Swedish-American entrepreneur and ecotourism pioneer, took delivery of MS *Lindblad Explorer*, the first vessel to be specifically commissioned for pleasure cruises to Antarctica.

MS *Explorer*. © Getty Images/Martin Harvey

Lindblad, who had previously organised a touristic cruise to the Antarctic Peninsula on board a chartered Argentine Navy ship in 1966, explained his motivations in these terms: 'I look down at the bottom of the map, unmarked by airline routes. Then I noticed that Antarctica wasn't even on the map. My enchantment with Antarctica had been so great since childhood that I wondered why I had never thought of it before. I was aware that the idea of setting up tours to that frozen continent would be tangled with complications. Going there might even be impossible. But inspired by koumiss, I boldly announced to everyone, "Our next exploratory tour will be to a place that isn't even on the map."'

Nicknamed 'the little red ship', the 73m (240ft) ice class MS *Lindblad Explorer* was built in Finland to carry 104 passengers. Lindblad's vision didn't stop at his commissioning of the *Explorer*, however. His model of expedition cruising, with shore landings on board inflatable boats and experts at hand to interpret sites of natural, scientific and historic interest, is still used by most Antarctic cruise operators today.

The Antarctic cruising industry grew spectacularly in the wake of the *Explorer*. Whereas Antarctica was once the preserve of explorers and scientists, it is now cruise passengers who represent the largest segment of visitors to the continent. According to the International Association of Antarctica Tour Operators, an organisation that manages the environmental impact of its members on Antarctica, more than 70,000 passengers, the majority from the United States, China and Europe, visited Antarctica in the 2019–20 season on board 70 vessels. These ranged from large cruise liners carrying many hundreds of passengers to small private sailing yachts.

Kay Van Horne, one of the rescued passengers when the MS *Explorer* sank in 2007. © Getty Images/Lyn Alweis

More recently, the original no-frills functionality of expedition-type vessels has given way to ever more luxurious and sophisticated ships offering everything from skiing and canoeing to rides on board helicopters and submarines.

As for 'the little red ship', she enjoyed an adventurous and sometimes tumultuous career, during which she changed hands on several occasions and twice ran aground, the passengers requiring rescue by the Chilean Navy. On 23 November 2007, she also acquired the illustrious status of being the first passenger vessel to run into an iceberg and sink in Antarctica. Although all of the passengers were once again rescued without harm by the Chilean Navy, the incident is often cited by those who campaign for tighter regulation of Antarctic tourism.

59

METEORITE

It is estimated that more than 17,000 meteorites impact the Earth annually. The best places to find meteorites are deserts, where organic activity and vegetation is minimal and meteorites lie more exposed and unaffected by erosion and other disturbances. Among deserts, it is the frozen wastes of Antarctica that have been the most fertile.

A vast majority of the at least 40,000 meteorites that have been found there have been recovered in blue ice areas where powerful katabatic winds and the direct conversion of ice into vapour (sublimation) removes all snow cover, leaving a hard and translucent blue ice surface. The meteorites found in these areas have either fallen from the sky and remained on the surface, or have gradually emerged from within the ice after being buried by snowfall at a distant point of impact, then transported by the flow of the ice mass and eventually reappearing. Regardless of which process lies behind the emergence of individual meteorites, blue ice fields offer a

Ursula Marvin searching for meteorites. © Smithsonian Institution Archives. Image # SIA2021-003907, Washington DC, United States

much higher number of meteorites than any other environment, in part, because the contrast of black against light blue make the specimens easier to find.

The first meteorite found in Antarctica was the 'Adélie Land meteorite', brought back by the Australasian Antarctic Expedition of 1911–14. It was discovered by Francis Bickerton in a shallow depression on the ice surface about 30km (18.6 miles) inland from the expedition's wintering hut at Cape Denison in East Antarctica.

The deliberate and co-ordinated search for Antarctic meteorites, however, only began in the 1970s following the reported discovery of three more meteorites by Soviet geologists near Novolazarevskaya Station in 1961–64, and the discovery of an additional nine meteorites by the 10th Japanese Antarctic Research Expedition in the Yamato Mountains, 250km (150 miles) inland from Showa Station, while carrying out glaciological work in 1969.

These early discoveries sparked an ongoing frenzy of interest for meteorite hunting in Antarctica, starting with Japan's 15th Antarctic Research Expedition, which recovered 663 meteorite samples in 1974. It was followed by the United States' Antarctic Search for Meteorites (ANSMET) programme established by geologist William Cassidy in 1976. Among the participants of the first ANSMET expeditions was Ursula Marvin, who had already been a member of the first team to study the Moon samples brought back by Apollo 11. Marvin participated in three ANSMET expeditions and went on to study Allan Hills A81005, the first lunar meteorite found on Earth, which was discovered in the Transantarctic Mountains in 1982.

Offering the possibility of increasing our understanding of the solar system at a tiny fraction of the cost of sending probes and robots to outer space, the quest for Antarctic meteorites has since been taken up by scientists from many other nations than the United States, Japan and Russia. These include a number of European nations, as well as South Korea, China, Australia and Turkey. Together, these nations and scientists contribute to keeping Antarctica as a frontier of exploration, both terrestrial and extraterrestrial.

'Yamato 691', discovered by the 10th Japanese Antarctic Research Expedition on 21 December 1969. © Japanese National Institute of Polar Research, Tokyo, Japan

60

PYRAMID TENT

While human structures in Antarctica have evolved a great deal over the course of the 20th century, one design that has held a continuous place is the pyramid tent, also known as the A-frame tent. Still used by several national Antarctic programmes, today's pyramid tents are only slightly modified versions of the ones used during the earliest inland expeditions.

Quick to assemble and fold, accommodating two to four persons, these tents, if properly secured, keep their inhabitants safe during the most extreme blizzard conditions. During his 1910–13 *Terra Nova* expedition, Scott expressed with great satisfaction 'What a wonderful shelter our little tent affords! We have just had an excellent meal, a quiet pipe, and fireside conversation within, almost forgetful for the time of the howling tempest without;—now, as we lie in our bags warm and comfortable, one can scarcely realise that "hell" is on the other side of the thin sheet of canvas that protects us.'

Little did Scott know that such a tent would later become his tomb, inside of which he and his companions still lie, enveloped by the Ross Ice Shelf as it slowly flows to the ocean.

Although the overall structure of pyramid tents has remained unchanged, many explorers and scientists have individualised their tents to best suit their needs. One such variation came from the 1969–70 American expedition to the McMurdo Dry Valleys, led by geochemist Lois Jones. This expedition, the first to be led by a woman, represented a major step forward in the inclusion of female scientists in Antarctic fieldwork.

Before Jones' expedition, the United States Navy and the National Science Foundation did not allow women to participate in Antarctic fieldwork. When Jones was eventually invited

'It is the tent'. Pyramid tent in which Robert Falcon Scott, Edward Wilson and Henry Robertson Bowers perished on their return from the South Pole. Photo by Tryggve Gran, 1912. © Scott Polar Research Institute, University of Cambridge, United Kingdom

Terry Tickhill standing by a tent at Vanda Camp in the Dry Valleys, Victoria Land. © Expeditions: Antarctica, 1969–70, Lois M Jones Papers, The Ohio State University, Byrd Polar and Climate Research Center Archival Program, United States

to go south, it was under the condition that she organise her own all-women's team. The team of four comprised Lois Jones, biologist Kay Lindsay, geology postgraduate student Eileen McSaveney and chemistry undergraduate student Terry Tickhill. The team primarily worked in support of Jones' research on the geochemistry of weathering and the saline cycle in southern Victoria Land, breaking rocks and collecting geological specimens. They were also among the first six women to visit the South Pole.

Years later, McSaveney recalled that, 'An elementary school had sent us some curtains to use in Antarctica ... They weren't terribly useful,

but we did string them on the outside our tents, and photograph them.' Upon her return to the United States, she delivered a series of lectures called 'The Only Tent with Curtains in the Antarctic'.

These curtains also poked gentle fun at the idea that these four women might miss the niceties absent in the harsh Antarctic environment. This photograph of curtains dressing up a pyramid tent demonstrates both the changes and continuities of Antarctic science and exploration. As the population of those allowed to visit Antarctica expanded and diversified, they still relied on the same architecture used by the continent's earliest explorers.

61

WHALE SKELETON

In 1972, world-renowned French explorer and marine conservationist Jacques-Yves Cousteau undertook an expedition to Antarctica, later immortalised by the 1976 documentary *Voyage to the Edge of the World*. He and his team observed and recorded the fauna and ice formations of Antarctica, recording some of the first film footage underneath icebergs and sea ice. On this voyage, Cousteau's ship, the *Calypso*, landed at Admiralty Bay, King George Island, to the north of the Antarctic Peninsula.

Once a site of shore-based Antarctic whaling, King George Island was littered with the remnants of that industry. Gathering bones scattered across the beach, Cousteau and his crew reconstructed the skeleton of a humpback whale to serve as a memorial to the whales killed through the first half of the 20th century, as well as to raise public awareness about the destruction caused by whaling. With the Brazilian Comandante Ferraz Antarctic Station later built just steps away, and landings from cruise ships ensuring a steady stream of visitors, it remains a poignant reminder of Antarctica's early history.

In the first half of the 20th century, the Southern Ocean whale fishery was the richest in the world. From 1909–18, over 3 million barrels of whale oil were produced, valued at over £20 million. In the ensuing years, the industry underwent a remarkable development, and in the single season of 1928–29 the output was over 1 million barrels valued at over £5.5 million. It is difficult to imagine a more brutal form of resource-based capitalism.

In 1926, during a busy day at Grytviken, the capital of the subantarctic island of South Georgia, where many whaling stations were located, biologist Alister Hardy painted the harbour as red with blood. British physician RB Robertson, who

A busy day at Grytviken whaling station, South Georgia, March 1926. By Alister Hardy. © National Maritime Museum, Greenwich, United Kingdom

Whale skeleton assembled by Jacques-Yves Cousteau on King George Island, 1972–73. © Sebastian Copeland

visited in the 1950–51 season, called it 'the worst administered place in the colonial possession of Great Britain, the most sordid unsanitary habitation of white men to be found the whole world over, and the most nauseating example of what commercial greed can do at the expense of human dignity...'

Several factors explain the gap in feeling over whales between the 1950s and Cousteau's visit to the former whaling grounds, some 20 years later in 1972–73. Whaling in the Southern Ocean was somewhat slowed in 1946 due to the International Whaling Convention (IWC), which sought to manage stocks responsibly. Shore-based whaling at South Georgia ended in 1965, due to a combination of fears regarding overfishing and the rise of pelagic whaling, which

saw whales processed on board factory ships, allowing a more economical way of capturing and rendering whales' by-products, as well as a means of avoiding British taxes.

Finally, in the 1960s, the work of marine conservationists such as Cousteau led to a cultural shift in public attitudes towards marine mammals. The album *Songs of the Humpback Whale*, produced by biologist Roger Payne in 1970, publicly demonstrated the elaborate vocalisations of whales. This album sold over 100,000 copies, helping to spawn the 'Save the Whales' movement. Other than the Japanese scientific whaling programmes, which continued until 2019, whaling in the Southern Ocean ended almost entirely after 1986, when a moratorium issued by the IWC came into effect.

62

BOARD GAME

Board games have been a fixture of Antarctic exploration since its earliest days. They became even more important with the first wintering expeditions; as the sun disappeared for months on end, games were a valuable means of fighting boredom. During the 1910–13 *Terra Nova* expedition, Apsley Cherry-Garrard described how 'In the matter of games it was noticeable that one would have its vogue and yield place to another without any apparent reason. For a few weeks it might be chess, which would then yield its place to draughts and backgammon, and again come into favour.'

Despite their many positive aspects, however, games have sometimes also become a source of tension, when friendly competition has turned into hostility. The worst such incident is said to have taken place at the Soviet Vostok Station in 1959. A scientist was so furious at having lost at chess that he picked up an ice axe and attacked his opponent. While some sources have affirmed that this resulted in murder, others have denied it. Whatever the truth, chess was banned from Soviet stations for years afterwards.

'Admiral Byrd's South Pole Game: "Little America"', Parker Brothers, 1934. © Byrd Polar Climate and Research Center, The Ohio State University, United States

Antarctic games, however, are not just those played in Antarctica. The 20th century saw the creation of a number of board games inspired by Antarctic exploration. One example was 'Admiral Byrd's South Pole Game: "Little America"'. Published in 1934 by Parker Brothers in association with the American explorer Richard Byrd, the box lid showed Byrd dressed in explorer gear, speaking via radio from Antarctica. The game was played on a very approximate cartographic depiction of the continent, and the aim was to follow an exploratory plane from New Zealand to the South Pole, overcoming numerous death traps along the way. The first to reach the pole was the winner.

Besides providing entertainment, 'Little America' served to enhance the heroic stature of Byrd and further secure his prominent place in the pop culture of the day. Indeed, the real winners were Byrd and Parker Brothers, who managed to sell 14,230 units of the game in its first year. These figures would probably have caught the attention of oil firm British Petroleum (BP), which published a game called 'Polaroute', a variation on snakes and ladders, to fundraise for the New Zealand Party of the 1955–58 Commonwealth Trans-Antarctic Expedition.

Paul-Émile Victor explains the rules of his game 'Conquête des Pôles' to a young boy, 1975. © Fonds de dotation Paul-Émile Victor, Courbevoie, France

The profits and publicity generated by 'Little America' may have also inspired Paul-Émile Victor to create his own board game, 'La Conquête des Pôles', released by the French publisher Fernand Nathan in 1975. Having built the foundations upon which France's Antarctic programme still stands today, Victor was something of a brand in his own right, offering all the marketing potential a publisher could hope for.

In contrast to 'Little America', which only focusses on Byrd's Antarctic exploits, however, 'Conquête des Pôles' reflects Victor's career in its bipolar dimension where, relying on a mixture of luck and strategy, the player is transported on a journey of exploration from the Arctic to the Antarctic, thus offering a basic education in the differences between the two regions.

63

PASSPORT

Antarctica is the only continent and territory on Earth without proprietor, national government or full time residents. While this implies that there is no such thing as an 'Antarctican', it does not mean that Antarctica is passport-free.

Personnel or visitors to Antarctic stations, for example, are often given the opportunity to have their passport stamped by station authorities to mark their visit. With the growth in Antarctic tourism and station visits by cruise ships, the stamping of passports has become more widespread, but because they are not governmental and can be read as an attempt to reinforce territorial claims, such stamps are increasingly frowned upon by border authorities.

A far more consequential connection between Antarctica and passports is manifest in the passport of the Republic of Argentina. On the back cover of the Argentine passport is printed what the Argentine authorities refer to as a 'bicontinental map' of Argentina, showing Argentina's South American territory, Las Islas Malvinas (the Falkland Islands), and its territorial claim in Antarctica. This 'bicontinental map' is not only present on Argentine passports but it also reflects a legal obligation for its citizens to include the Argentine Antarctic territory when drawing and printing maps of their country.

This obligation is intended to remind the international community that despite signing the Antarctic Treaty of 1959, Argentina still asserts its legitimacy over the Antarctic Peninsula region, including territories also claimed by Chile and the United Kingdom. Indeed, this geopolitical perspective is similar to the one that led Argentina, then governed by military dictator Leopoldo Galtieri, to seize the subantarctic island of South Georgia and the Falkland

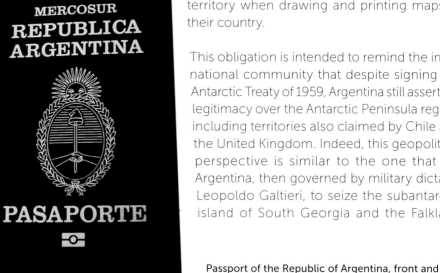

Passport of the Republic of Argentina, front and back. © Wirestock, Inc./Alamy

Islands (Las Malvinas) in 1982. And it is also the same assertation that led Argentina to orchestrate the first human birth on the continent on 7 January 1978, when a heavily pregnant Silvia Morella de Palma was taken down to Argentina's Esperanza station in order to give birth to her son Emilio Palma. Repeated at least six times between 1978 and 1983, this Argentine initiative triggered a Chilean response that saw the births of at least three babies on Chilean Antarctic bases in 1984–85, during the Augusto Pinochet regime.

Much less serious in its potential long-term ramifications is artists' Lucy + Jorge Orta's tongue-in-cheek 'Antarctica World Passport'. With a blue design reminiscent of many real passports, the Ortas' Antarctic passport was printed in significant numbers and, in the artists' words, 'may be issued to any person wishing to become a citizen of the world, allowing them to travel freely. The Antarctic nationality will proportion rights but will also request in return that citizens take responsibility for their actions.'

This statement extends the ideals of the Antarctic Treaty in its framing of Antarctica as a global commons that belongs to all the citizens of the world and stands as a symbol of peace and harmony. In this, it is reminiscent of a number of initiatives to design new Antarctic flags that have in common the desire to evoke Antarctica as an idealistic realm apart: one whose isolation and internationalism somehow resists the complexities and cacophony of the wider world.

'Antarctica World Passport' by artists Lucy and Jorge Orta, 2015. © Studio Orta, Paris, France

64

AEROPLANE WRECKAGE

At 12.30pm on 28 November 1979, Air New Zealand's Antarctic sightseeing flight TE901 made its last radio contact with the United States' McMurdo Station, located at the foot of the southernmost active volcano on Earth, Mount Erebus.

On board the DC-10 were 20 crew and 237 passengers, mostly from New Zealand, but also Japan, the United States, the United Kingdom, Canada, Australia, France and Switzerland. They had gathered at the windows, admiring and photographing the Antarctic landscape beneath them. Among them was Peter Mulgrew, who had previously taken part in the 1955–58 Commonwealth Trans-Antarctic Expedition. He had agreed to replace his friend Edmund Hillary as a lecturer on the flight.

Mount Erebus, photographed from an aircraft, 1974–75.
© Antarctica New Zealand Pictorial Collection

Air New Zealand had started Antarctic sightseeing flights two years earlier and they had become routine. Lasting 11 hours, they looped passengers from New Zealand to Antarctica without landing on the continent.

All seemed to be going smoothly as the pilots flew at a low altitude over the Ross Sea and McMurdo Sound coastline in order to provide the best possible views. Then, at 12.49pm, the ground proximity warning systems triggered alarms in the cockpit; a few seconds later flight TE901 crashed catastrophically into the lower slopes of Erebus, killing everyone on board.

When the aircraft stopped responding, a search operation was launched from McMurdo. At 9pm, about half an hour after the DC-10 would have consumed its last litres of fuel, Air New Zealand informed the press that they believed the aircraft had been lost. The wreckage was eventually located at 12.55am, 12 hours after the impact. Strewn over an area the size of 20 football pitches, the crash site was a dark scar across the immaculate snow.

The loss of TE901 remains the biggest single disaster in both New Zealand and Antarctic history. The event and its aftermath left deep wounds, not just among the bereaved families, but across New Zealand and internationally. Among the most traumatised were the 60-person recovery team of police officers, mountain rescuers, pathologists and dentists deployed to the crash site in the hours and days following. For more than ten days, they camped amid the wreckage in unimaginably difficult conditions. Underequipped, with little water and no change of clothes, they worked non-stop to recover all possible human remains.

Air New Zealand initially attempted to blame Captain Thomas J Collins and his crew. The enquiry, however, concluded that the airline itself was partly to blame and had produced 'an orchestrated litany of lies' to hide the crew's lack of specialised training for flying over Antarctica, and that they had been briefed with a different flight path to the one programmed into the plane's computer. Combined with the low cloud cover that hung over Mount Erebus that day, blurring any differentiation between snow and sky, this resulted in the pilots mistaking their

Piece of fuselage wreckage from Air New Zealand Flight TE901, which remains on the slopes of Mount Erebus. Photo by Phil Reid, 2004. © Antarctica New Zealand Pictorial Collection

position and dropping altitude on a trajectory that led them straight into the volcano's flanks.

While Air New Zealand ceased operating sightseeing flights to Antarctica, they are still conducted by other airlines. Because the crash site was on a flowing glacier, a memorial was placed on a nearby rock.

65

SKIDOO

Skidoos — motorised tracked toboggans capable of carrying one or two individuals and hauling Nansen sledges — have been the primary means of travel for Antarctic field parties since the 1970s. Relatively lightweight and easy to maintain, their introduction to Antarctica meant that dog teams were no longer necessary for long traverses or fieldwork.

Decades before skidoos, motorised vehicles first travelled to Antarctica with Ernest Shackleton's 1907–09 *Nimrod* expedition. Among the expedition's supplies was an Arrol-Johnston motor car, an early pickup truck with a flatbed for cargo. For traction, Shackleton built a set of cogged wheels and fitted runners under the front wheels, hoping these would enable the vehicle to travel over soft snow. In January of

George J Dufek, commander of the United States' Operation *Deep Freeze III*, examines a motor sledge brought to Antarctica during Ernest Shackleton's *Nimrod* expedition, 1907–09. © Getty Images/Bettmann

1908, 'off the car went with the throbbing sound which has become so familiar in the civilised world, and was now heard for the first time in the Antarctic'. But their delight was short-lived. Though this car was used for five journeys of significant length, it was not functioning sufficiently well to accompany the men on their South Pole journey.

For the 1910–13 *Terra Nova* expedition, Robert Falcon Scott also brought motorised sledges to Antarctica with high hopes: 'Apart from such help I am anxious that these machines should enjoy some measure of success and justify the time, money, and thought which have been given to their construction.' Within days of landing, one had already fallen through the sea ice and was lost. Though the team made several attempts to use motorised sledges on their journeys, by November Scott observed: 'So the dream of great help from the machines is at an end!'

There were several other expeditions in the first half of the 20th century that attempted to draw upon motorised transport with varying degrees of success. These include Jean-Baptiste Charcot's 1908–10 *Pourquoi-Pas?* expedition, Wilhelm Filchner's 1910–12 *Deutschland* expedition, the 1934–37 British Graham Land Expedition, the 1947–48 Ronne Antarctic Research Expedition, and Richard Byrd's

Charles Burton rests on a Ski-Doo during the Arctic portion of the Transglobe Expedition, 1982. © Getty Images/Brendan Monks/Daily Mirror/Mirrorpix

first three expeditions. The first mechanical Antarctic traverse was made during the 1949–52 Norwegian-British-Swedish Expedition.

The 1959 invention of the Ski-Doo opened the market for the mass production of versatile snowmobiles that could be used by any traveller in snowy remote areas. This particular brand became so popular that in some communities 'skidooing' became a verb to describe all kinds of snowmobile travel.

Skidoos gave valuable service to British adventurer Ranulph Fiennes' 1979–82 Transglobe Expedition, the first expedition to make a longitudinal circumnavigation of the Earth using surface transport. On the polar portion of this expedition, each skidoo dragged 15m (49ft) tows as a safety measure in areas that they suspected had crevasses.

Echoing the Heroic Age expeditions that inspired it, the Transglobe Expedition also took on geopolitical significance during the Falklands War of 1982, when the sovereignty dispute between Argentina and the United Kingdom reached its tipping point. While skidoos continue to be associated with epic expeditions such as Fiennes', today they are used in almost every aspect of Antarctic logistics.

66

TELEPHONE

Antarctica is sometimes imagined as a place beyond the reach of communication technologies, but this perception has been inaccurate for over a century. While the 1911–14 Australasian Expedition, a pioneer in this field, got little use out of their wireless telegraph due to the deteriorating mental health of its operator, Sidney Jeffryes, Antarctic visitors have long had an array of communication technologies including radios, telegraphs, telephones, and now satellite and digital communications. Indeed, it did not take long for communication technology to be literally built into the Antarctic landscape, and in the near future, a planned undersea fibre-optic cable may even be deployed between New Zealand and the United States' McMurdo Station, physically connecting Antarctica to the rest of the world.

The telephone shown here belonged to New Zealand's Vanda Station in Victoria Land, on the shore of Lake Vanda, and served as part of a communication system between the base's different huts. The telephone cables, bundled with power cables, were strung overhead at roof level, connecting the huts together. This particular telephone includes an image of a woman's eye staring out from the receiver, attached to the telephone as a joke, speaking to the history of how the Antarctic was conceived as a masculine space.

Photographs of women were ubiquitous to Antarctic architecture, in part because of women's physical absence from the continent through much of the 20th century. Long absent from their sweethearts, sisters and mothers, some men yearned for their domestic lives and the sound of women's voices, chatting for extended periods over the radio with women back at home and even reading women's magazines. In contrast, however, images of nude or scantily clad women adorned both the living and working quarters on Antarctic stations. As one commentator put it, for many years, rather than physically being in Antarctica,

'Women are only a figment of the imagination and made in two dimensions...'

At Vanda Station, rituals of masculinity were commonly practised. In 1984, *Sports Illustrated* described the tradition of the Royal Vanda Swimming Club, which included rules like '1. No togs allowed'; '4. Complete immersion must be achieved'; '6. No restriction on photography'. Although the author conceded that some women had joined the swimming club, the continent is still one of 'straightforward male virtues... The unwritten Vanda rule is simple: A gentleman, presented with the opportunity to swim, swims.' And as these men stripped down to just their footgear before submerging, they were overseen by 'an old swimming-safety poster displaying a buxom beauty and the legend EVERYBODY NEEDS A BUDDY'.

Thus, just as telephones allowed intercommunication on bases, the cut-outs of women signalled that this was a place for men only. The presence of women would, at best, be a distraction and at worst, disrupt the culture, rituals and sense of fun on these stations. Today, men still greatly outnumber women at Antarctic

research stations, but many national Antarctic programmes are prioritising greater gender diversity, shaping Antarctica into a space for all.

Black Bakelite telephone installed at New Zealand's Vanda Station in 1969. © Harrowfield Collection/ Canterbury Museum, Christchurch, New Zealand

67

DOBSON SPECTROPHOTOMETER

The Dobson spectrophotometer was one of the earliest instruments used to study atmospheric ozone, a stratospheric gas that shields Earth's surface from the sun's harmful ultraviolet radiation. The Dobson, as it has become commonly known, measures the total ozone by measuring the relative intensity of the ultraviolet B (UVB) radiation that reaches the Earth and comparing it to that of ultraviolet A (UVA) radiation at ground level. Using the ratio between UVA and UVB radiation on the ground, it determines how much ozone is present in the upper atmosphere to absorb the ultraviolet C (UVC) radiation.

In 1985, British Antarctic Survey scientists Joseph Farman, Brian Gardiner and Jon Shanklin published an article in *Nature* that shook the world. Entitled 'Large losses of total ozone in Antarctica reveal seasonal ClO_x/NO_x interaction', the article used ozone measurements gathered with Dobson spectrophotometers at the United Kingdom's stations at Halley Bay and the Argentine Islands since 1957 to demonstrate

Joseph Farman, Brian Gardiner and Jon Shanklin in the British Antarctic Survey ozone lab. Photo by Chris Gilbert, 2002–03. © UKRI-BAS. Reproduced courtesy of the British Antarctic Survey Image Collection, Cambridge, United Kingdom (ref. 10007093)

that there was serious depletion of ozone in the southern hemisphere – what became known as the ozone hole.

Combined with American chemist F Sherwood Rowland's contemporaneous research demonstrating that the chlorofluorocarbons (CFCs) used in refrigerators, cooling systems and some aerosol propellants contribute to ozone depletion, Farman, Gardiner and Shanklin's *Nature* article revealed that the widespread use of synthetic chemicals had led to a 40 per cent decline in southern hemisphere ozone levels within a decade.

The group's discovery helped to bring about the 1987 Montreal Protocol, an international treaty to protect the ozone layer and to phase out the production of CFCs and other ozone-depleting gases. This was the first universally ratified treaty in the United Nations' history. Kofi Annan, former secretary-general of the United Nations, described the protocol as 'perhaps the single most successful international agreement to date'. The Montreal Protocol continues to serve as an inspiration for international environmental protection negotiations and treaties, including the Intergovernmental Commission on Climate Change, which convened the following year.

This proactive response since the 1980s has resulted in the progressive shrinking of the ozone hole, which is predicted to recover by the end of the 21st century.

Dobson spectrophotometer installed at Halley VI station, 2012. © James Morris

68

DINOSAUR FOSSIL

Fossil records reveal that in the deep past, when it was located further to the north as part of the Gondwana supercontinent, Antarctica was rich in flora and fauna. Throughout the 20th century, many fossils, some of them holotypes unique to the region, were used to reconstruct ancient Antarctic landscapes and seascapes. It was in the final decade of the century, however, that perhaps the most charismatic discovery was made: the Antarctic landmass was once home to large, carnivorous dinosaurs.

In 1991, American palaeontologist William R Hammer and geologist David Elliot were excavating outcrops near the Beardmore Glacier in the Trans-Antarctic mountains when Elliot's team came across the remains of a dinosaur and notified Hammer's team. Within a month, Hammer excavated 2,300kg (2.5 tons) of fossil-bearing rock, recovering over 100 fossil bones. In the May 1994 issue of *Science*, Hammer described his findings as the fossil remains of an early Jurassic crested theropod. He named this new discovery *Cryolophosaurus ellioti*; *cryo* for cold, *lopho* for crested, *saurus* for lizard, and *ellioti* for the dinosaur's finder.

Cryolophosaurus was a large predator, currently the largest known Early Jurassic theropod, living between 200 and 180 million years ago. Hammer estimated that it was between 6–7m (19.7–23ft) in length. Since this particular skeleton has been estimated to be a sub-adult, however, the adult *Cryolophosaurus* could have been even larger.

Other dinosaur fossils have been found in Antarctica since this first discovery. In 1990 and 2011, Hammer discovered the fossil remains of two sauropodomorphs in the Central Trans-Antarctic Mountains, later named *Glacialisaurus hammeri* in his honour. In 2019, the Field Museum in Chicago opened a major travelling exhibit highlighting dinosaurs and dinosaur hunters in Antarctica, including the 'harrowing logistics and excavation work as scientists uncover remarkable fossils from one of the most isolated environments on Earth'. The search for Antarctic fossils continues today, as a new generation of geologists use dynamite, shovels and growing knowledge of Antarctic landscapes to uncover and identify the still unknown creatures that made the region their home millions of years ago.

Palaeontologists Steve Krippner and Bill Hickerson excavating at Mount Kirkpatrick, 1991. © William Hammer, Augustana College, Rock Island, United States

Cryolophosaurus femur in situ in Antarctica, prior to excavation, 1991.
© William Hammer, Augustana College, Rock Island, United States

69

T-SHIRT

As winter darkness descends upon Antarctica, the Southern Ocean freezes over, surrounding the continent with a rampart of sea ice that isolates it from the rest of the world. Seen from space, it appears as though Antarctica has doubled in surface area.

Until recently, anyone who had not left Antarctica before the onset of winter had to sit out the long, dark winter months and wait for the sun to rise again in the spring. For Adrien de Gerlache's *Belgica* expedition of 1897–99, the first to winter in the Antarctic, this interminable wait resulted in a chaotic mix of scurvy, mental illness, breakdowns in command, and death.

Indeed, stories of delirium, assault and possibly murder, using everything from hammers to axes and perhaps even poison, have long been integral to the folklore of wintering in Antarctica. Both McMurdo Station's Chapel of the Snows and Argentina's Almirante Brown station have been the scene of winter arson attacks by discontented personnel.

There have also been amazing stories of survival. In 1961, Leonid Rogozov, a Soviet physician wintering at Novolazarevskaya Station, successfully removed his own appendix. Many national Antarctic programmes now require that a person's appendix is removed before

they can visit the continent. In 1998, American physician Jerri Nielsen diagnosed herself with breast cancer and treated her condition with airdropped chemotherapy supplies and hormone

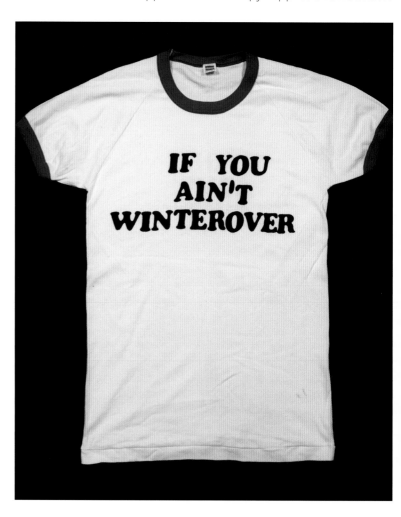

medication until she could be airlifted out of the United States' South Pole station.

As Antarctic expeditions developed better infrastructure and occupations for 'winteroverers', however, winter also yielded new pleasures, for example in the forging of strong community bonds and a sense of 'Antarctic belonging' as expressed in the festive celebration of the winter solstice or the contemplation of the aurora australis. Journalist Michael Cross noted in 1991 – before women were able to winter at British stations – that Antarctic winters were 'a special time for the chaps'.

As expressed by this T-shirt from the mid-1980s, wintering in Antarctica provides status, differentiating those who have had the experience from those who have not. Among the winteroverers, however, even more exclusive groups include the South Pole station's 300 Club, reflecting the number of people who have survived a temperature difference of more than 300°F (149°C) by waiting for a day when the outside temperature falls below -100°F (-73°C), taking a sauna at 200°F (93°C), then running outside and around the Ceremonial South Pole naked. Or indeed the unofficial most-winteroverer club, comprising several individuals who have spent at least a dozen winters on the continent, the record currently believed to be 15.

Today, around 1,000 individuals winter in Antarctica each year. They mostly oversee the maintenance of research stations, as well as scientific observations. Although still mostly male, the number of female winteroverers has risen steadily in recent decades.

In the last few years, however, Antarctica's winter isolation has been encroached upon by a number of midwinter resupply flights to American and Australian stations using large C-17 cargo planes. These flights are a source of regret for those nostalgic for the time when being cut off from the world meant exactly that – whatever the cost.

Back and front of winteroverer T-shirt, 1980s. © Harrowfield Collection/ Canterbury Museum, Christchurch, New Zealand

70

JOIDES RESOLUTION

Our understanding of Antarctica's glaciation lies at the centre of questions regarding the Earth's geological and climatic history. One of the keys to reconstructing this history is the retrieval of sediment cores from regions of the Southern Ocean near the continent. The *JOIDES Resolution*, or *JR*, plays a central role in this effort.

Paradoxically for a vessel used to research climate history, the *JR* was built as an oil exploration vessel in 1978, before being converted into a scientific research platform for the Ocean Drilling Programme (ODP) in 1985. It was then that she was renamed after James Cook's HMS *Resolution*, the first vessel to sail south of the Antarctic Circle.

Operated by Texas A&M University and funded by the National Science Foundation, the *JR* is the main United States contribution to what has now become the International Ocean Drilling Programme. This is the longest-running and most successful international collaboration in the Earth sciences, joining together scientists and agencies from more than 20 nations.

The *JR*'s defining feature is her drill tower, or derrick, arising from the centre of the ship and reaching as high as a 20-storey building. Combined with dynamic thrusters positioned beneath her hull to keep her in a fixed position while drilling, and a moon pool through which drilling rods and marine exploration devices can be lowered directly into the ocean from within the ship, the derrick lies at the centre of the *JR*'s exceptional capabilities as a research vessel.

To date, the *JR* has undertaken more than 160 expeditions, visiting nearly 1,000 drill sites across all of the world's oceans. Thanks to a modernising refit in 2007–08, she is now able to drill as deep as 8,235m (5.1 miles) beneath the ocean surface. So far, she has extracted a phenomenal 2,500 sediment and geological cores, totalling more than 300km (186 miles) in length.

The extraction, classification and initial analysis of cores on board the *JR* is made possible with a team of 50 scientists and some 65 crew members. Operations run 24 hours a day, both on deck and in the ship's extensive laboratory and core storage spaces. Cores are recorded and analysed on macro and micro scales, taking into account both their physical properties and their geochemistry.

Tina van de Flierdt and Saiko Sugisaki studying sediment cores extracted from the Ross Sea, 2018. © Justin Dodd, Northern Illinois University, DeKalb, United States

The *Joides Resolution* sailing into the Ross Sea for the start of the International Ocean Drilling Programme Expedition 374, January 2018. © Rob Dunbar, Stanford University, Palo Alto, United States

Since 2010, the *JR* has undertaken three expeditions and retrieved cores from more than 30 locations south of the Antarctic Circle, providing precious information on how Antarctica's ice sheets have grown and melted over the past 34 million years. The two most recent expeditions focused more specifically on the history of the West Antarctic Ice Sheet (WAIS), which is the most vulnerable within the context of human-induced climate change. Through mapping the WAIS' past advances and retreats, scientists have shed light on how it might respond to the Earth's current warming: a question of the highest global relevance.

71

RED APPLE HUT

The environmental protection and preservation of Antarctica – what one historian has called 'the greening of Antarctica' – is a relatively recent phenomenon. The past five decades have seen a growing number of environmental non-governmental organisations (NGOs) advocating for the protection of different aspects of both Antarctic fauna and the ecosystem as a whole. Among the first NGOs to concern itself with the region was Greenpeace.

World Park Antarctica banner being raised at Cape Evans, Antarctica, 1987. © Greenpeace/Andy Loor

Greenpeace's Antarctic campaign reached its apogee with the signing by 33 nations of the Convention on the Regulation of Antarctic Mineral Resource Activities (CRAMRA) in 1988. CRAMRA was designed to manage the exploitation and development of Antarctica's mineral resources, and had necessitated six years of painful secret negotiations. It was in response to such threats to Antarctica's delicate environment that Greenpeace challenged what it regarded as the overly exclusive Antarctic Treaty System (ATS) and proposed instead to make Antarctica a 'World Park' whose preservation could be managed by the United Nations or another globally inclusive organisation.

To gain traction for the idea of an Antarctica World Park, Greenpeace purchased a helicopter-equipped vessel, the MV *Gondwana*, and in 1987 established its World Park Base at Cape Evans, next to Robert Scott's wintering hut during the *Terra Nova* expedition. The World Park Base stayed open for five years and closed in 1991. It remains among the most expensive campaigns ever staged by an environmental organisation.

The World Park Base was the central element of a multifaceted campaign during which Greenpeace drew attention to a host of environmental hazards around the continent. Most significant among these was France's construction site for a gravel airstrip capable of receiving intercontinental aircraft at its Dumont d'Urville research station, a project that required the bulldozing together of islands and the disruption of penguin rookeries. For these campaigns, Greenpeace deployed a 'red apple' hut that became emblematic of its efforts.

Although Antarctica was never made a World Park, Greenpeace's campaigning did result in France's abandonment of its airstrip project and the 11th-hour non-ratification of CRAMRA, one of the greatest achievement in the entire history of Greenpeace. Joining forces with other organisations and personalities, such as Jacques-Yves Cousteau, the World Wildlife Fund, the

Antarctic and Southern Ocean Coalition and the Wilderness Society, Greenpeace also contributed significantly to convincing Bob Hawke and Michel Rocard, the Australian and French prime ministers, to withdraw from what Cousteau referred to as the 'stupid' CRAMRA convention.

Helped by the 1989 disaster of the sinking of the *Exxon Valdez*, which underlined the devastating effects of 37,000 tons of crude oil being spilled into the ocean off the coast of Alaska, and the grounding of the *Bahía Paraíso* that same year, which saw 510 tons of diesel oil leak into the sea along the Antarctic Peninsula, the French and Australian withdrawal from CRAMRA struck a terminal blow to the convention. It also set the stage for the negotiation and 1991 signing of the Protocol on Environmental Protection to the Antarctic Treaty, which replaced CRAMRA and banned all mining activities in Antarctica.

Greenpeace 'red apple' hut. © Greenpeace

72

PENGUIN TAXIDERMY

Penguins are one of the most charismatic animals on Earth; a major attraction at any natural history museum is the taxidermy penguin. While capturing, killing, stuffing and displaying penguins has often been in service of science, their public display, such as in this diorama, often comprises elements of the theatrical and the entertaining.

The exoticism, behaviour, ease of anthropomorphism and 'cuteness' of penguins are particularly adept at feeding the imagination. In Antarctica, besides being objects of study, penguins were sources of curiosity and amusement; it is still common for the personnel at research stations to journey to penguin colonies in their free time. Penguins' relative lack of fear made them easy to capture. Nan Brown, who lived on the subantarctic island of South Georgia in the 1950s, recalled a guest bringing a penguin to a dinner party as a prank. She herself adopted one as a pet. The pet penguin "loved to be petted, patted, and played with and, where other penguins fought and struggled when helped, he happily submitted to being picked up and cuddled."

Penguins are of course also immensely popular with the general public. Richard and Florence Atwater's children's novel *Mr. Popper's Penguins*, published in 1938, about a group of Antarctic penguins who star in a theatre circus act, remains widely read by young Americans and was loosely adapted into a feature film in 2011. Children's films starring penguin characters are box office draws and range from the *Chilly Willy* cartoon series, which aired 1953–72, to the 1995 animated romance-adventure film *The Pebble and the Penguin*, to the computer animated blockbuster franchise *Happy Feet*, launched in 2006.

Nature films on penguins are also well received. In 2019, Disneynature released *Penguins*, which blended footage of Adélie penguins with narration to create a coming-of-age story. National Geographic and BBC Earth also frequently show films on the lives of penguins. The French documentary *March of the Penguins*, which focused on the breeding habits of emperor penguins, became a global phenomenon on its release in 2005. It was shortlisted and won prizes at the BAFTA Awards, the César Awards and the Academy Awards.

'Clissold and Anton with an Emperor penguin', British Antarctic *Terra Nova* expedition, 1910–13. Photo by Herbert Ponting. © Scott Polar Research Institute, University of Cambridge, United Kingdom

Diorama of taxidermied emperor penguins, Canterbury Museum, Christchurch, New Zealand. From Anne Noble's *Ice Blink* photographic book and series (published by Clouds, New Zealand, 2011). © Anne Noble

In *South*, a silent documentary film on the Imperial Trans-Antarctic Expedition, director Frank Hurley, fearing that he lacked the footage of Antarctic fauna that audiences demanded, returned to South Georgia in 1917 after being rescued from Elephant Island so that he could shoot additional footage of Antarctic wildlife.

Most people will never visit Antarctica. Yet, through depictions of penguins in books and films, their presence in zoos, and their display as taxidermies in natural history museums, both young and old can see the star residents of the Antarctica, learn about the region's landscape, and let their imaginations run.

73

SLEDGE

The early history of Antarctic exploration is well populated with the exploits of heroic adventurers looking to secure their place in history by pulling sledges into the unknown, pushing themselves to their physical limits while achieving geographical firsts.

Since the Second World War, most of those who spend a significant amount of time in Antarctica are either scientists or support staff for national Antarctic programmes. Some, however, still go there in search of adventure, challenging both the landscape and themselves while setting records and traversing remote territories.

American Ann Bancroft is an example of a prominent Antarctic adventurer. After multiple skiing expeditions to the Arctic, in 1992–93 she led the first all-woman expedition to ski to the South Pole and, in 2001, she and Norwegian explorer Liv Arnesen became the first women to ski across the Antarctic continent.

The Commonwealth Women's Antarctic Expedition, 2009. © Felicity Aston

Crossing Antarctica remains an extremely difficult and arduous task. Like Heroic Age explorers, Bancroft and Arnesen towed their supplies on sledges, which they harnessed to their bodies and pulled on skis or on foot. In Bancroft's words, 'When you have to drag everything you decide to bring with you in a sled, you deliberate long and hard about what you "need" to bring. Our sleds become our universe.'

This photograph (right) of Bancroft, taken at Ulvetanna Peak in Queen Maud Land during her and Arnesen's 2000–01 trek across the continent, shows her pulling her sledge while climbing up onto the Antarctic Plateau. Made from fibreglass, her loaded sledge weighed 124kg (273lb), more than twice her own 59kg (130lb). Inside her waist belt were pads that could be taken away or added as she lost weight during the course of the expedition.

The line between scientist, explorer, adventurer and tourist is a blurry one. Several scientific expeditions have contained a high degree of adventurism. Likewise, many attempts to set records have yielded important scientific observations. Even a solo journey across portions of Antarctica, relying on your endurance and survival skills, can, under some circumstances, officially classify you as a tourist. Felicity Aston, an adventurer and former meteorologist at Britain's Rothera Antarctic Station, once commented on the apparent incongruity of reaching the South

Pole on skis, only to be shuttled into an area designated for tourists.

Since 2001, Bancroft and Arnesen have continued leading expeditions in challenging regions around the world, using their platform to draw attention to global issues such as climate change and clean water access.

Ann Bancroft pulling her sledge in Queen Maud Land, 2000–01. © Ann Bancroft Foundation, Saint Paul, United States

74

GEOLOCATOR

For the French poet Charles Baudelaire, the albatross was 'the prince of the clouds', the most legendary of all seabirds.

Eighteen of the more than 22 recognised species of albatrosses live in the Southern Ocean. The biggest is the wandering albatross. With a wingspan that can exceed 3m (9.9ft), it can live more than 60 years and fly up to 1,000km (621 miles) in a single day. Like most species of albatrosses, it spends the majority of its life at sea, only landing on remote outcrops of the Southern Ocean during the breeding season.

Today, albatrosses are under threat, with some species on the verge of extinction as a consequence of incidental mortality (bycatch) in fisheries, invasive alien species at colonies and disease. Their brutal decline in numbers is made worse by their slow reproductive rate, taking up to ten years or more to reach sexual maturity, with some species, including the wandering albatross, breeding only every other year.

The tagging of albatrosses with geolocators was pioneered in the late 1990s and early 2000s. These tiny devices record ambient light and make it possible to estimate a bird's location twice per day by applying astronomical algorithms to the timing of sunset and sunrise. This allows scientists to measure the scale to which albatrosses have been affected by human activities, particularly fishing, as well as to better understand their habitat preferences and how

A wandering albatross on Bird Island, fitted with a geolocator. Photo by Richard Philips. © UKRI-BAS. Reproduced courtesy of the British Antarctic Survey, Cambridge, United Kingdom

Light-level geolocator tag for tracking Southern Ocean albatrosses. © Courtesy of Richard Philips, the British Antarctic Survey, Cambridge, United Kingdom

Engraving by Gustave Doré of a scene from the Coleridge's *The Rime of the Ancient Mariner*, 1877.
© Getty Images/Duncan1890

climate change influences their distributions, year-round.

Despite deep-rooted maritime superstitions about a curse that befalls those who kill an albatross, their killing is nothing new. As early as the second voyage of James Cook, when he ventured south of the Antarctic Circle, the expedition's naturalist, Georg Forster, 'shot some albatrosses and other birds, on which we feasted the next day, and found them exceedingly good'.

Cook's account of this voyage possibly also inspired the Romantic poet Samuel Taylor

Coleridge to write *The Rime of the Ancient Mariner*, published in 1798 and arguably the first piece of Antarctic literature. In this poem, Coleridge recounts the story of a sailor needlessly killing an albatross with his crossbow as it appeared out of the fog. As punishment by his crew, the sailor is forced to wear the body of the albatross around his neck and do penance after the souls of the rest of the crew have themselves been claimed by death.

For some, *The Rime of the Ancient Mariner* has become an allegory for the destruction that humans have brought to Polar Regions.

75

SHIPPING CONTAINER

Since their patenting in 1956, shipping containers have become as omnipresent in Antarctica as anywhere else. Indeed, as a continent where all equipment and supplies must be imported, Antarctica is more dependent on containers than practically any other region. Used to transport everything from canned foods to helicopters, containers are most often delivered to Antarctica by ship, but sometimes also by large cargo aircraft. Once in Antarctica, they are often unloaded onto large ski sledges. This allows them to be hauled across the ice by tracked vehicles, sometimes over thousands of kilometres when resupplying inland stations.

Transport, however, is not the only use for containers in Antarctica. Thanks to their low-cost functionality, they have been adapted for a variety of uses, in particular as convenient building blocks for Antarctic architecture. Among the earliest examples of an Antarctic station entirely constructed from containers was East Germany's Georg Forster Station, built in 1976. The ten containers were insulated, equipped with doors and windows, and generally pre-fitted as laboratories, power units and sleeping and living quarters before being shipped to the Antarctic and assembled.

East Germany's Georg Forster Antarctic station, the first to be built from shipping containers in 1976. © Hartwig Gernandt, courtesy of the Alfred Wegener Institute, Bremerhaven, Germany

Ten years later, as many as 82 pre-fitted containers were used to construct Italy's two-storey Zucchelli Station, with 42 containers used for personnel accommodation and the remainder for support, logistics and science. Containers were also used by the Chinese Antarctic programme to construct the original buildings of its Great Wall 'Chángchéng' Station on King George Island in 1985, and of its Zhongshan Station in East Antarctica in 1989.

While some of these early buildings have since been decommissioned, in 2009 and 2012 Germany and India chose to use containers as the primary building blocks

Lutz Fritsch's 'Library in the ice' assembled in a container at Germany's Neumayer research station in 2004. © Lutz Fitsch, courtesy of the Alfred Wegener Institute, Bremerhaven, Germany

of their respective Neumayer III and Bharati research stations. Although Bharati is larger, comprising 134 containers and providing 2,500sq m (26,910sq ft) of heated living and working space compared to Neumayer's 1,850sq m (19,913sq ft), they share a similar approach in design. Both are raised above the surface on stilts and comprise an external structure that envelops the containers. These envelopes provide a more aerodynamic and aesthetic appearance to the stations, while shielding the internal structures and providing better insulation.

Smaller-scale container structures are also common in Antarctica. Some are fixed units, often located in the vicinity of stations and housing specific scientific experiments that should not be disrupted by station activities. Others are mobile containers that can be hauled into the field to serve as accommodation, laboratories, workshops and other uses on a temporary basis. Supplementing or replacing tents altogether, containers provide much more comfortable living and working spaces during longer scientific fieldwork and traverses: Antarctica's answer to the caravan.

Some of the most creative uses of containers in Antarctica are as greenhouses, chapels, or as the 'library in the ice' created by the German artist Lutz Fritsch: a cosy 700-book library assembled in a green container within walking distance of Neumayer-Station III. There, station personnel can seek refuge and tranquillity, exploring new literary horizons while looking out at the expanse of the ice shelf. With their alien and impermanent appearance, shipping containers conjure an image of Antarctica as an ongoing frontier.

76

SOUTH POLE MARKER

Planted about 100m (110 yards) in front of the United States' Amundsen-Scott South Pole Station is a semicircle of 12 flags belonging to the original signatories of the Antarctic Treaty. At the heart of the semicircle is a red-and-white pole with a reflective metallic sphere positioned on top. Known as the 'Ceremonial South Pole', this sphere does not mark the actual geographical South Pole. Located another couple of hundred metres away, the geographic South Pole is marked by a simple metallic pole on top of which sits a sculpted bronze plaque or sculpture that is changed annually.

The Geographic South Pole, located at latitude 90° South, is one of the two points where the axis of rotation of the Earth intersects with its surface. The other is the Geographic North Pole, located at 90° North. The Geographic South Pole should not be mistaken for the South Magnetic Pole, which is the changeable point where the Earth's magnetic field lines are directed vertically upwards. Although usually considered fixed, the Geographic South and North Poles are not entirely stationary. They move around a tiny fraction of a degree as the Earth wobbles very slightly during its rotations.

Whereas the Geographic North Pole is located towards the middle of the frozen Arctic Ocean, the Geographic South Pole is located in the central region of the ice-covered Antarctic continent. While it is easier to plant a marker at the Geographic South Pole than on the drifting sea ice or seabed at the North Pole, the glacial flow of the Antarctic ice sheet means that each year the South Pole marker travels 10m (32.8ft) north of 90° South.

Today, the Ceremonial South Pole is intended to embody Antarctica's and the South Pole's international dimension, and is used as a backdrop for expeditioners and other visitors to photograph themselves at the pole. Less frequently visited, the marker pinpointing 90° South is repositioned on the first day of each year by United States Antarctic Program personnel to compensate for the 10m (32.8ft) it has travelled over the previous year. The repositioning is commemorated with a small ceremony that comprises changing the bronze marker designed and fabricated annually by overwinterers in the station workshop. All the old markers are exhibited in a cabinet inside the South Pole Station.

Ceremonial South Pole Marker. Photo by Deven Stross.
© Courtesy of the United States Antarctic Program Photo Library, United States

During the long dark winter, when temperatures plummet to -60°C (-76°F), the South Pole marker is sometimes also used by overwinterers for a uniquely Antarctican ritual of initiation: running naked around the South Pole.

Markers for the Geographic South Pole: 2010, 2012, 2022, 2004. By Forest Banks, Liesl Schernthanner, Andrea Dixon and Pete Koson. © Courtesy of the United States Antarctic Program Photo Library, United States

77

ICE CORE

Antarctica is often described as a climate archive. Thanks to the extraction and analysis of ice cores from the Antarctic ice sheet, it is possible not only to reconstruct climate fluctuations going back around a million years, but also to better understand what drove these fluctuations. Although past climate can be read in other natural manifestations such as tree rings, coral reefs and sediment cores, the information contained in ice cores is particularly wide-ranging and precise. It extends from carbon-dioxide concentrations to volcanic ash, to droughts, and even evidence of fluctuations and evolutions in industrial manufacturing.

Ice cores are retrieved using augers originally designed for geological drilling. These consist of drill barrels equipped with helical blades on the outside. The barrel drills down into the ice, wrapping itself around a core of ice. Once filled, the barrel is extracted from the borehole with the ice core inside it. Modern augers can extract up to 6m (19.7ft) of ice at a time, at a rate of about 35m (114.8ft) a day. Cores are then removed from the barrel and cut into 1m (3.3ft) sections before being archived in special cold storage facilities outside of Antarctica.

The first Antarctic ice cores were retrieved during the 1949–52 Norwegian-British-Swedish Antarctic Expedition. The longest reached a depth of 100m (330ft), and all were analysed in situ, with particular attention given to the changing crystalline structure of ice at different depths.

The ice core extracted in 1966–68 at the United States' temporary Byrd Station on the West Antarctic Ice Sheet was the first to extend right through from the surface to the bedrock 2,164m (7,100ft) below. When analysed in parallel with the Camp Century ice core extracted from the Greenland ice sheet in 1963–66, the Byrd ice core revealed important parallels between the climate fluctuations experienced by the northern and southern hemispheres.

Perhaps the most important ice cores in Antarctic history, however, were those extracted by Soviet scientists at Vostok Station on the East Antarctic Ice Sheet and analysed by French scientists in the mid-1980s and 1990s. These culminated in a 420,000-year climate record covering four glacial

Four ice coring rigs at the Soviet Vostok Antarctic station, 1984. © Michael Creseveur/Fonds Lorius/CNRS Photothèque

Richard Nunn, assistant curator of the National Science Foundation's Ice Core Facility, holding a segment of a core in the archive freezer. © National Science Foundation, United States

cycles, and resulted in a series of momentous papers in *Nature*. Providing evidence of the correlation between atmospheric temperature and the concentration of greenhouse gases in the atmosphere, these papers reinforced the argument that human activities were increasing global atmospheric temperature and became some of the most cited by climate campaigners.

The Vostok findings were confirmed with the extraction of newer ice cores, the deepest being the Japanese Dome Fiji ice core, and the EPICA ice core at Dome Concordia. The EPICA ice core recovered nearly 800,000 years of climate history across eight glacial cycles.

Projects such as Beyond EPICA are now underway to recover an ice core that contains more than a million years of climate history. This would shed light on a time when the Earth's glacial cycles abruptly doubled in length for reasons not fully understood.

78

STELLAR AXIS

Since the earliest human incursions into the region, most of our artistic engagement with the Antarctic has been through drawing, painting and photography. Since the start of the 21st century, however, new art forms have emerged on the continent. These are no longer about documenting or expressing Antarctica, but instead about using it as a backdrop for sculpture or other more ephemeral installations and performances.

Among the handful of artists who have produced such works are Stephen Eastaugh, Richard Long, Pierre Huyghe, Chris Drury and Alexander Ponomarev. The most ambitious installation thus far, however, was artist Lita Albuquerque's *Stellar Axis: Antarctica*, created in December 2006 on

'Sirius' from Lita Albuquerque's *Stellar Axis: Antarctica* ephemeral land art installation, 2006. Photo by Jean de Pomereu. © Lita Albuquerque

the vast Ross Ice Shelf, at the foot of the active volcano Mount Erebus, 30km (18.6 miles) from the United States' McMurdo Station.

Albuquerque's work belongs to the land art movement that began in the 1960s with the great earthworks of Walter De Maria, Michael Heizer and Robert Smithson. Her intention with *Stellar Axis: Antarctica* was to create a large-scale celestial map mirroring the constellations in the sky above Antarctica on 21 December, the day of the summer solstice, when 24 hours of daylight envelop the continent and the stars are invisible.

Albuquerque's inspiration was to 'bring the stars down to Earth' through the precise arrangement of 99 ultramarine blue spheres of different sizes, each one representing a star and its perceived luminosity. Working with astronomer Simon Balm, she positioned the spheres across the ice to reflect the invisible constellations above, reminding us that stars continue to shine during daylight, and that Antarctica's ethereal nature makes it a privileged conduit between heaven and Earth.

Supported by the United States National Science Foundation's Antarctic Artists and Writers Program, *Stellar Axis: Antarctica* was so creatively and logistically complex that it took three years of

Lita Albuquerque's *Stellar Axis: Antarctica* ephemeral land art installation, 2006. Photo by Jean de Pomereu. © Lita Albuquerque

planning before the project reached Antarctica. After two weeks of installation, during which Albuquerque and her team had to anchor the spheres into the ice strongly enough for them to withstand an Antarctic storm, the result was a breathtaking but ephemeral 'modern day Stonehenge' some 150m (492ft) in diameter.

Albuquerque invited scientific and logistical personnel from McMurdo Station to take part in a choreographed procession on the day of the solstice. Under her guidance, the participants walked through *Stellar Axis* in a concentric spiral, echoing our illusion of stars circling in the sky as we see them from the rotating Earth. In compliance with Antarctic Treaty regulations, the installation was then dismantled, with no trace left behind.

79

ICESAT

Satellites have been surveying and monitoring changes in Antarctica's climate, ice and ocean since the 1970s. Built by NASA and launched in 2003 as part of its Earth Observing System, ICESat was the first satellite designed to measure the effects of climate change across both Polar Regions, especially relating to cloud cover, ice sheet and sea ice thickness.

Positioned in a near-polar orbit at an altitude of approximately 600m (1,970ft), ICESat's sole instrument was a Geoscience Laser Altimeter System that beamed lasers down to Earth to measure small variations in elevation as it passed repeatedly over the same regions. Originally intended to operate for three to five years, ICESat remained functional for seven years before being retired in 2010, at which point it burned up on re-entering the Earth's atmosphere.

The significance of the data collected over Antarctica during the ICESat mission cannot be overstated, especially considering that the Antarctic ice sheet contains more than 90 per cent of the Earth's surface fresh-water, or enough to raise sea levels by 60m (197ft) if it were to melt entirely. Although ICESat showed that certain sectors of the Antarctic ice sheet recently gained in mass and depth due to local increases in snowfall, it also confirmed that, overall, the Antarctic ice sheet is losing volume and contributing to global sea level rise. This is especially pronounced in West Antarctica, where much of the ice sheet rests on bedrock that lies below sea level and is thus particularly prone to the rising temperature in the surrounding Southern Ocean.

ICESat was eventually succeeded by NASA's ICESat-2, launched in 2018. Like its predecessor, ICESat-2 carried a single instrument, an Advanced Topographic Laser Altimeter System, and had the mission to continue the measurement of ice sheet elevation and sea ice thickness, as well as recording land topography, vegetation density and cloud cover.

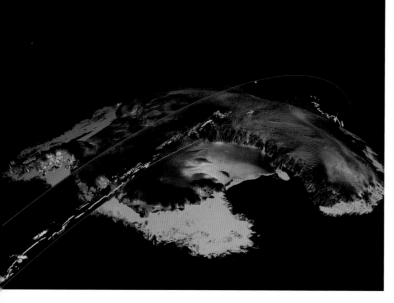

ICESat data swath over Antarctica showing ice sheet elevation and clouds. © NASA/Goddard Space Flight Center Scientific Visualization Studio, RADARSAT mosaic of Antarctica (Canadian Space Agency)

Other polar and ice observation satellites include the European Space Agency's CryoSat-2, which was launched in 2010. Still operational

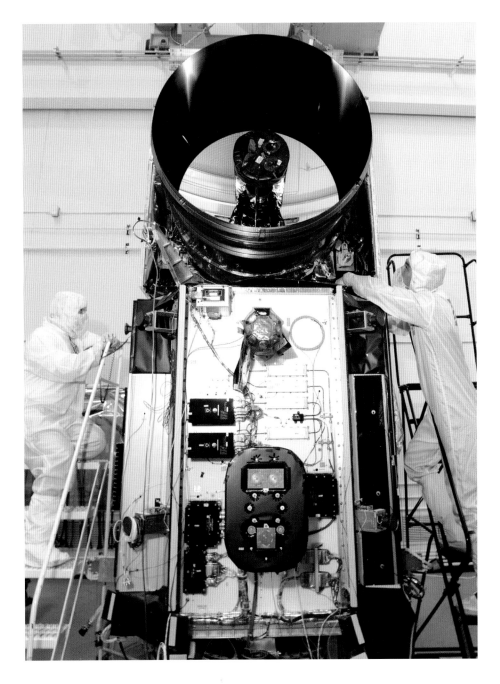

Geoscience Laser Altimeter System, ICESat satellite, launched by NASA in 2003. © Courtesy of NASA Goddard Space Flight Center, Greenbelt, United States

today, CryoSat-2 also has a mission to measure changes in the volume and dynamics of polar ice sheets, as well as the thickness and extent of sea ice. Unlike ICESat and ICESat-2, however, CryoSat-2 uses a Radar Altimeter (not a Laser Altimeter) to detect tiny variations in ice elevation and sea level. Together, these satellites help us to better understand and predict the future of cryospheric environments and their impact beyond the Polar Regions.

80

HYDROPONIC VEGETABLES

A major staple missing from Antarctic diets in the early years of its exploration was fresh food, especially fruit and vegetables. Despite the constraints of frozen ground and winter darkness for months on end, however, explorers and scientists set their minds to finding solutions, with Antarctica more recently becoming a testing laboratory for growing fruit and vegetables in space.

As early as the 1901–04 *Discovery* expedition, physician and botanist Reginald Koettlitz grew mustard, cress and other vegetables, experimenting whether defrosted Antarctic soils could support life. The experiment was a success and his mustard and cress contributed to staving off the ever-threatening scurvy. Since then, more than 40 plant production facilities

Member of the King Sejong Station, working in the station greenhouse, 2020. © Korea Polar Research Institute, Incheon, South Korea

have operated and experimented in Antarctica. The proliferation of plant production facilities ultimately contributed to fears regarding human impact on Antarctic environments.

Hydroponic fruit and vegetables, King Sejong Station, 2020. © Korea Polar Research Institute, Incheon, South Korea

These fears contributed to the drafting of the Protocol on Environmental Protection to the Antarctic Treaty, which came into effect in 1998. The Madrid Protocol, as it is better known, now prohibits the introduction of non-native soils or animals to Antarctica. As a result, the only permissible way of growing fruit and vegetables in Antarctica is hydroponically – a method of horticulture that replaces soil with mineral nutrient solutions diluted in water.

In recent decades, several national Antarctic programmes have set up hydroponic greenhouses. For example, at South Korea's King Sejong Station on King George Island, a 'plant factory' was installed inside a shipping container in 2009. Lined with polyurethane insulating panels, this facility produces an average of more than 1kg (2.2lb) of fresh vegetables per day. Harvests include peppers, lettuce and tomatoes, providing the 18-member overwinterers with fresh salad at least once a week. A similar horticultural plant was set up at South Korea's Jang Bogo Station in Terra Nova Bay in 2014, operating within the main building of the station.

Other countries operating hydroponic green-houses in Antarctica include India, New Zealand, China, Russia, Italy, Poland and Germany. The United States even established a hydroponic greenhouse at its South Pole station. In addition to providing fresh food for the stations' residents, scientists use the facilities to research how their food-growing techniques might be applied in even more inhospitable environments, like the depths of the ocean or outer space. The facilities also serve as a place for mental well-being, where relaxing amid plants and warmth provides a welcome respite to the cold starkness of the Antarctic environment.

81

TELESCOPE

The qualities that coalesce to make the interior of Antarctica the most hostile of terrestrial environments are the same as those that make it the best location for astronomy. Extreme cold makes the air drier, with less atmospheric emission of infrared light. Twenty-four-hour darkness in the winter eliminates daily variations in temperature, which in turn reduces air currents and increases atmospheric stability. Geographic remoteness means there is almost no air pollution. High altitude combined with a thinner atmosphere at the poles presents a clearer view of the cosmos. Finally, Antarctica is accessible to astronomers at a fraction of the cost of sending a telescope into space.

Although the use of astronomical telescopes in Antarctica dates back to the Heroic Age, the first sustained Antarctic astronomical programme was started by American astronomers at the South Pole, altitude 2,8355m (9,300ft), in the early 1990s. Designed to measure the Cosmic Microwave Background (CMB) and observe the earliest moments of the universe, the current South Pole Telescope was inaugurated in 2007 and has been equipped with three successive and increasingly sensitive cameras. In 2019, as part of the Event Horizon global network of telescopes, it played a key role in capturing the first image of a supermassive black hole, described as a 'one-way door out of the universe'. This was one of the greatest collaborative achievements in the history of astrophysics.

AST3-2 0.5m (1.6ft) telescope at China's Kunlun Station, Dome Argus, 2015. Photo by Duan Dewen. © Fugia Du. Courtesy of Fugia Du and the PLATO-A observatory

Other telescopes and astronomical instruments installed on the Antarctic ice sheet include a multicolour PAIX photometer launched at the Franco-Italian Concordia station at Dome C in 2007, followed by the SuperDARN radar installed in 2018, intended to investigate space weather and the Earth-Sun relation. Dome C, altitude 3,233m (10,607ft), will soon be home to an instrument intended to measure the distortions of the CMB frequency spectrum. Japanese scientists are currently working to install a 2m (6.6ft) infrared telescope at Dome F, altitude 3,810m (12,500ft).

The most promising site for Antarctic astronomy, however, is the Dome Argus region, which includes the highest point of the Antarctic ice sheet, altitude 4,093m (13,428ft), with average winter temperatures of around -70°C (-94°F). Already the site of the Chinese Kunlun Station, the location has been described as the best optical astronomical site on Earth and has hosted a number of small optical telescopes jointly operated by Chinese and Australian astronomers since 2007. More recently, China has installed two infrared Differential Image Motion Monitors at Dome A to further determine the night-time observation potential of the site, and aims to install larger 2.5m (8.2ft) and 5m (16.4ft) optical infrared telescopes. China's ultimate aim is to install both an 8m (26.2ft) optical telescope and a 15m (49.2ft) submillimetre telescope.

Astronomers from the United States and Australia have also been evaluating Ridge A, about 160km (100 miles) distant from Dome A. Described as the perfect 'eye in the storm' from which all winds flow out and none flow through, it appears to be the closest you can get to space and still be on Earth. In the competitive field of Antarctic astrophysics, where location and size play such an important role, it seems that things are only just beginning.

South Pole Telescope and BICEP (Background Imaging of Cosmic Extragalactic Polarization) experiments at the United States' Amundsen-Scott South Pole Station, 2019. © Shaun O'Boyle

82

CHAPEL

While it is often perceived that an inherent conflict exists between science and religion, this has been widely discredited by scholars. Even on the continent most associated with science, religion is also present. Indeed, Antarctica itself continues to be a source of spiritual wonderment for many visitors.

While an undocumented number of shrines and other permanent or temporary places of worship have been established within the confines of Antarctic research stations, stand-alone religious buildings in Antarctica are currently all Christian. These include St Volodymyr Chapel, a Ukrainian Orthodox chapel at the Vernadsky Research Base; St Ivan Rilski Chapel, an Eastern Orthodox church at Bulgaria's St Kliment Ohridski Base; Chapel of Our Lady of the Snows, located in an ice-cave at Argentina's Belgrano II station; and the Chapel of St Mary Queen of Peace, a Roman Catholic chapel located at Chile's Villa Las Estrellas.

Interior of the Trinity Church, a Russian Orthodox church at Bellingshausen Station, King George Island. © Getty Images/Bloomberg

Illustrating the place, experiences and concerns of other faiths in Antarctica, various rabbis have written treatises about adhering to Jewish religious laws in the Polar Regions, where the sun rarely rises or sets completely. In 1996, Australian environmental scientist David Hornstein, stationed at New Zealand's Scott Base, celebrated Passover by having a traditional Seder, and recalled for *Tablet* magazine the moment that 'We went to open the door of the New Zealand scientific base during the Seder to welcome Elijah the Prophet. It was about 75 degrees Fahrenheit inside the base, but outside it was absolutely freezing and when we opened the door, the outdoor temperatures caused sheets of white mist to fly into the room in front of all my colleagues. I can assure you that we were the only ones in the world that year that invited Elijah to visit an Antarctic Seder!'

While there are no mosques in Antarctica, the construction of Pakistan's Jinnah Antarctic Station in 1991 made Islam a permanent presence on the continent, forcing adaptations for practice of Ramadan, which relies on sunrise and sunset to determine fasting schedules. Jordanian adventurer Mostafa Salameh, who skied to the South Pole in 2016, prioritised the practice of his religion even on the ice. As he explained in a 2015 interview: 'I will still do my 5 prayers a day. I can do it inside the tent if it's windy and very cold outside. I always carry a very light Prayer Carpet with me.'

Chapel at Chile's Arturo Prat station. Photo by Jean-Erick Pasquier. © Getty Images/Gamma-Rapho

McMurdo's non-denominational Chapel of the Snows also holds meetings for a variety of religions including Bahá'í Buddhism and the Church of Jesus Christ of Latter-day Saints, as well as non-religious groups such as Alcoholics Anonymous. In the 21st century, many Antarctic visitors have also embraced attending religious services held online. While there is a maritime saying that 'Beyond 50 degrees south there is no God', the pervasiveness of religious custom in Antarctica seems to suggest otherwise.

83

OPTICAL MODULE

Buried kilometres deep within the ice beneath the Geographic South Pole is the largest scientific instrument in Antarctica and one of the biggest on Earth. Known as IceCube, it is a cosmic observatory, or telescope, measuring more than 1cu km (35,315cu ft) in volume and consisting of over 5,000 Digital Optical Modules (DOMs). Each about the size of a beach ball, the DOMs are attached to 'strings' lowered and frozen into 86 boreholes arranged in a hexagonal grid.

The purpose of IceCube is to detect subatomic particles known as neutrinos. Often described as ghost particles, neutrinos have no electric charge and almost no mass. This allows them to travel through space and matter, including galaxies and vast magnetic fields, as if there was nothing there. Created by violent and distant astrophysical events such as exploded stars and the Big Bang, neutrinos hold a key to understanding these phenomena.

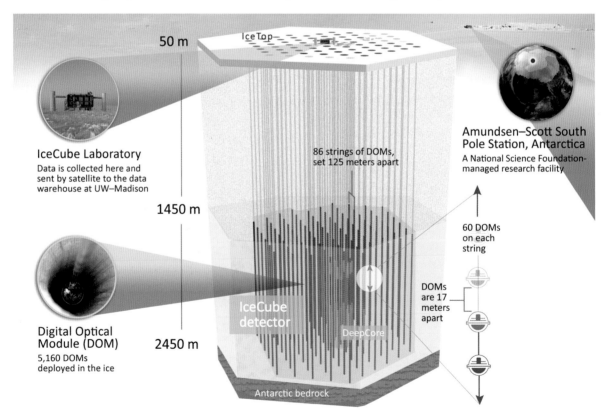

50 m

IceTop

IceCube Laboratory
Data is collected here and sent by satellite to the data warehouse at UW–Madison

86 strings of DOMs, set 125 meters apart

Amundsen–Scott South Pole Station, Antarctica
A National Science Foundation-managed research facility

1450 m

60 DOMs on each string

Digital Optical Module (DOM)
5,160 DOMs deployed in the ice

2450 m

IceCube detector

DeepCore

DOMs are 17 meters apart

Antarctic bedrock

3D diagram of IceCube neutrino observatory beneath the South Pole.
© IceCube, National Science Foundation, United States

Despite their abundance (trillions pass through us every second), the only moment when neutrinos become observable is when one collides with a proton. This is extremely rare, but when it happens it creates another particle called a muon, which continues in the same path as the neutrino and produces a conical streak of blue light known as Cherenkov radiation. By observing the angle and direction of the streak, astrophysicists are able to retrace the trajectory of the neutrino, and ultimately to pinpoint and study the cosmic event that created it billions of light years away.

One way to detect neutrino-proton collisions is to monitor a very large volume of transparent and stable matter, and among the best places on Earth to find such an environment is deep within the Antarctic ice sheet. There, compressed by its own weight, the ice is sufficiently transparent to allow the DOMs frozen inside to detect streaks occurring in their vicinity.

One of the Digital Optical Modules that make up the IceCube neutrino observatory at the Geographic South Pole. Photo by Robert Schwartz. © IceCube, National Science Foundation, United States

The construction of IceCube began in 1996 with the deployment of just 19 strings. With a rising cost of nearly $300 million USD, it has been expanded ever since in order to increase its performance. In the context of Antarctica, where science and geopolitics are often intertwined, some argue that IceCube is an ideal tool for the United States to accredit its station and presence at this most symbolic of locations, the South Pole. For others, it stands out as inspirational, cutting-edge science at the ends of the Earth.

Where Antarctica was once 'another world', with IceCube the continent has become a privileged vantage point from which to observe even more distant 'other worlds'.

84

PATCHES

For a continent that belongs to no one, Antarctica incites a particularly strong sense of belonging and pride at having 'been there'. While it is by no means the only one, a particularly visible expression of this is an embroidered patch.

The existence of embroidered patches goes at least as far back as antiquity, when they were used to mend holes in clothing. More recently, their widest use has been by military organisations as a means to assert rank and regiment. Then in the 1960s, they were appropriated by countercultures who used them to identify with and promote anti-establishment ideals.

Although they were more often printed or engraved on paper labels, crockery and silverware, the kind of logos that were later made into embroidered patches first appeared in Heroic Age expeditions at the beginning of the 20th century. It was only after the Second World War, however, that large United States Navy expeditions, such as Operations *Highjump* and

Deep Freeze, introduced a fully-fledged patch culture to Antarctica.

Particularly suited to stitching on parkas and other thick Antarctic clothing, the use of patches rapidly expanded beyond the Navy and permeated all aspects of human involvement in Antarctica. Among the more traditional patches were those produced for scientific programmes, exploring expeditions, ship and air support crews, station support staff and international research collaborations. These figured everything from ships and aircraft to representations of individual stations, land features, flags and penguins. While the appetite for such patches was once primarily American, they have been adopted by both countries with long Antarctic histories and more

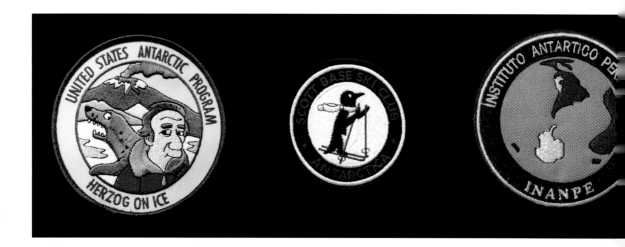

recently by newer signatories of the Antarctic Treaty, like India, South Korea, Malaysia, Ecuador and Peru, as a mark of their growing ambitions and commitment to the continent's culture.

Away from the governmental and institutional, Antarctic cruise operators have also produced patches, either to sell as souvenirs and trophies to passengers or to promote their brand. Non-governmental organisations have also made use of patches to campaign for the causes they defend. For example, Greenpeace's Antarctica World Park patch features an orca and rainbow, and Sea Shepherd's patch comprises a skull, crook and trident.

The most humorous Antarctic patches, however, have been those produced by smaller Antarctic communities to promote some of the quirkiest aspects of Antarctic life and culture. Leaders in this field are the New Zealanders and their patches for everything from the Scott Base's exclusive swimming, ski, golf and rugby clubs, to ones commemorating Antarctic traditions and events. Examples of such traditions include romantic encounters on the ice or art projects, such as a patch memorialising the filming of *Encounters at the End of the World* on which

director Werner Herzog is made to resemble Bart Simpson.

As well as demonstrating a person's belonging to a specific Antarctic 'club' or project, patches serve as a physical affirmation of an individual's connection with the region. Perhaps surprisingly, this has led to the recent trend in producing and stitching patches featuring fake Antarctic expeditions and research programmes on to outdoor clothing by brands seeking to give their clothing a sheen of Antarctic authenticity.

Patches received by Jean de Pomereu on his visits to Antarctica. Representing Instituto Antártico Peruano, New Zealand's Scott Base Ski Club, the 25th Chinese National Antarctic Research Expedition, the United States Antarctic Program, the International Polar Year 2007–08, and the filming of Werner Herzog's *Encounters at the End of the World*. © Courtesy of Jean de Pomereu

85

S.A. *AGULHAS II*

While 29 countries currently maintain Antarctic stations, a more elite group owns and operates ice-breaking ships. Some countries, like the United States, Norway and Russia, also use ice-breaking ships in domestic capacities as Arctic nations. Most of the ice-breakers operated by non-Arctic nations, are also utilised across both Polar Regions for logistical support and oceanographic research. For some governments, the significant investment required to build and maintain these vessels is at least in part justified by their ability to demonstrate their country's strategic commitment to Antarctic research, as well as their ability to support Antarctic stations without relying on the ice-breaking capacities of other nations.

An example of this balancing act between research, logistics and strategic interest is South Africa's successive ice-breakers. The nation's first ice-breaking research ship, S.A. *Agulhas*, was built in 1978 to support the South African National Antarctic Programme, replacing its first Antarctic supply vessel, the 1,573-tonne *R.S.A.* The S.A. *Agulhas* was succeeded in 2012 by the 100-berth

South Africa's Antarctic supply vessel, *R.S.A.*, 1970–71. Photo by Eugene Els. © Antarctic Legacy of South Africa Archive, Stellenbosch, South Africa

S.A. *Agulhas II*, which, unlike its predecessor, is equipped with onboard laboratories, cranes and deck-handling systems that can be used for oceanographic, biological and environmental and even marine archaeological research. For instance, in 2022 the *Agulhas II* was used to search for the wreck of Ernest Shackleton's *Endurance*.

While South Africa does not maintain any territorial claims on the Antarctic continent, it has long been geopolitically interested in Antarctic affairs. Cape Town is one of the five cities in the world typically identified as an 'Antarctic Gateway', a place through which many people transit on their way to Antarctica. Additionally, South Africa possesses two small islands in the subantarctic, Marion Island and Prince Edward Island, formally claimed by the British Empire and annexed by South Africa in 1947–48. Soon after annexation, South Africa established a research station on Marion Island, which it continues to operate in parallel to a station at the still-British subantarctic Gough Island, first established in 1956. It was during the International Geophysical Year of 1957–58 that South Africa launched its National Antarctic Expedition (SANAE) in Queen Maud Land. All three stations are now supported by the S.A. *Agulhas II*.

S.A. *Agulhas II*. Photo by Hermann Luyt, APECSSA competition, 2018.
© Antarctic Legacy of South Africa Archive, Stellenbosch, South Africa

Like all Antarctic science, South Africa's commitment to Antarctic engagement has had a political dimension. In a 1925 address to the South African Association for the Advancement in Science, former prime minister Field Marshal Jan Smuts argued that South Africa should be increasingly involved in Antarctic affairs, particularly in the field of meteorology. Establishing South African meteorological stations on the continent and its subantarctic islands would be a 'reunion of the scattered members of the ancient mother continent-Gondwanaland' from which Antarctica began to detach about 180 million years ago. On the other hand, echoing global condemnations of the South African apartheid system in the second half of the 20th century, many members of the Antarctic Treaty System protested South Africa's exportation of such policies to the Antarctic.

Dedicated to singer-songwriter and anti-apartheid activist Miriam Makeba and captained by Knowledge Bengu, the child of a Durban township who became South Africa's first Black ice pilot, the S.A. *Agulhas II* speaks to a South Africa that is grappling with its past and moving strongly into the future.

86

KRILL OIL CAPSULES

The exploitation of the Southern Ocean has been a central element of Antarctic history and continues to be an important aspect of human engagement with the region today. After the excesses of the 19th and 20th centuries, which saw the near extinction of certain species of seal and whales, attention turned to fish, squid and krill.

Krill are shrimp-like crustaceans found across all of the world's oceans. Of the 85 known species of krill, the most abundant is *Euphausia superba*, or Antarctic krill, of which 400 million tons can be found in the Southern Ocean. That makes *Euphausia superba* the most abundant species on Earth. While little is known about their migration around Antarctica, there is evidence that swarms of Antarctic krill can extend across more than 400sq km (154sq miles), enough to influence the carbon cycle and modify currents as they move through the water column.

About the length of a thumb, Antarctic krill can live up to six years and feed off phytoplankton, (microscopic single-celled plants) that they scrape from the underside of sea ice or consume as it drifts just below the ocean surface. A key component of the Southern Ocean food chain, krill are themselves an important food source for crabeater, fur and leopard seals, most species of whales, icefish, squid, and seabirds such as penguins and albatrosses.

Since the first Antarctic krill fishery was established by the Soviet Union in 1972, the crustacean has also been harvested by humans and become an increasingly important source of protein for farmed seafood, poultry and livestock. Rich in omega-3 fatty acids, krill oil is also a popular food supplement for humans and domesticated animals, with a growing demand from the billion-dollar agri-food and health supplement industries.

In response to the growth in krill harvesting, catch quotas were first introduced in 1993 within the framework of the Convention of

Krill. © Getty Images/Roger Tidman

WeightWorld Antarctic krill oil.

the Conservation of Antarctic Marine Living Resources (CCAMLR), whose mission is to regulate the wider fishery of the Southern Ocean. This has resulted in the recent banning of krill harvesting in large areas around the Antarctic Peninsula and the creation of 'buffer zones' around penguin colonies. It also lies at the centre of international negotiations to extend the number of Marine Protected Areas around the Southern Ocean. Quotas, however, have not prevented countries like Norway, Russia and China from introducing larger and larger special-

purpose krill trawlers to replace the less efficient multi-purpose trawlers of the past. Nor does the CCAMLR help to mitigate the threat to krill presented by the acidification of the Southern Ocean resulting from the increase in carbon dioxide in the atmosphere, or to slow decline of sea ice on which krill depend for phytoplankton.

With the krill oil industry projected to continue its double-digit growth, it is no exaggeration to say that the balance of the entire Southern Ocean depends on the preservation of krill stocks.

87

PEE FLAG

Planting flags as a mark of precedence or territorial appropriation is central to Antarctic history. Expeditions have carried and flown flags on board ships, sledges and other means of transport, as well as planting them along newly discovered coastlines, on the summit of mountains, and at significant geographical and magnetic locations.

In 1898, Carsten Borchgrevink's *Southern Cross* expedition took 500 Union Jacks with which they planned to claim Antarctic regions for the British Empire. The next two decades famously saw flags planted at the geographic and magnetic South Poles during the Antarctic expeditions of Ernest Shackleton, Roald Amundsen and Robert Falcon Scott. In 1912, Nobu Shirase's expedition planted the first Japanese flag on the continent. Particularly prolific in flag planting, the 1929–31

British Australian and New Zealand Antarctic Research Expedition saw Douglas Mawson and his men make five separate landings on Antarctica's shores, each time photographing themselves as they planted Union Jacks and took possession of the territory for the empire. In 1943, as part of a sovereignty dispute over the Antarctic Peninsula, the United Kingdom's Operation *Tabarin* established a base at Deception Island, removing Argentine flags and replacing them with the Union Jack. Over the years, Argentina, Chile and the United Kingdom routinely destroyed or stole each other's flags on the peninsula. Examples abound.

Flags, however, are not only used for colonial expansion in Antarctica. They are also employed to mark safe passages or danger zones across the ice, or – as is playfully exhibited in Anne Noble's 'Piss Poles' series – to mark a single designated location where campers are asked to pee or empty pee bottles when working in the field. In order to concentrate the pollution, the location of these pee patches are recorded for reference, but stay behind when camps are folded and flags removed. Eventually buried within the ice mass, these patches remain frozen as they begin their glacial-pace journey towards the ocean.

Photographed in 2008 at various deep field research locations during her United States

Cheering the flag on the summit of Proclamation Island, 13 January 1930, British Australian and New Zealand Antarctic Research Expedition, 1929–31. Photo by Frank Hurley. © Getty Images/Royal Geographical Society

176

'Piss Pole #4'. From Anne Noble's *The Last Road* photographic book and series (published by Clouds, New Zealand, 2014). © Anne Noble

Antarctic Program Artist residency, Noble's 'Piss Poles' is a playful exploration of colonialism, the marking of territory, and the taking of ownership through urination, like many species of mammals, or through flag planting, like humans. In highlighting the irony of combining these two practices, peeing and flag planting, Noble poses serious questions about the ongoing legacy of the Heroic Age of Antarctic exploration, and what exploration necessarily implies in terms of leaving traces, both physical and imaginative.

Anne Noble's 'Piss Poles' exemplify the growing humanistic and social science interest in the Antarctic as a continent that was never just the reserve of peace and science.

88

AQUATIC ROVER

The start of permanent large-scale research programmes in Antarctica is contemporaneous with humanity's first incursions into space. In 1957, the Soviet Union launched the first satellite, igniting the space race with the United States. This led to the establishment of the international space station and the development of national space programmes. For most of this period, the extreme environments of the Antarctic, as well as its status as an international commons for scientific research, turned the region into an analogue for outer space.

Starting in the 1960s, research into extremophiles living on the hostile Antarctic continent, particularly in the McMurdo Dry Valleys, helped to reveal what life might look like on other planets. In the 1970s, microbiologists Roseli Ocampo-Friedmann and Imre Friedmann travelled to Antarctica's Darwin Mountains, where they discovered unicellular blue-green algae living inside the rocks that tolerated the cold and, in the summer, would rehydrate and photosynthesise. This research suggested that endolithic life forms could survive in Martian environments and could ultimately be used to terraform Mars. NASA later referred to their work when the *Viking 1* spacecraft landed on the planet in 1976 and undertook biological experiments to find evidence of life on Mars. Studying Antarctic landscapes to better understand extraterrestrial environments continues to this day.

Antarctica's climate, topography, atypical seasons and degree of isolation means that the Antarctic is frequently used to develop preliminary research on the equipment and protocols that will one day be used in extraterrestrial exploration. In 2011, for instance, scientists and engineers travelled to Marambio Island, along the Antarctic Peninsula, to test a newly developed pressurisable North Dakota eXperimental-1 spacesuit, developed for possible future human field operations on Mars. In 2019, the Buoyant Rover for Under-Ice Exploration, developed at NASA's Jet Propulsion Laboratory to explore the frozen oceans on Jupiter's moon Europa and Saturn's moon Enceladus, was tested at Australia's Casey Station.

In addition to technologies, Antarctica serves as a key site for studying human behaviours and capabilities in extraterrestrial environments. At the

Buoyant Rover for Under-Ice Exploration. Photo by Kevin Hand. © NASA/JPL-Caltech, Pasadena, United States

North Dakota eXperimental-1 (NDX-1) spacesuit, 2011. © Courtesy of Pablo de León. University of North Dakota, Grand Forks, United States

Concordia Station, for instance, the European Space Agency annually sponsors medical doctors to carry out studies on the effects of isolated, confined and extreme environments on humans. In 2019, science and exploration in these two regions coincided when American astronaut Christina Hammock Koch was launched from the Baikonur Cosmodrome on a Soyuz spacecraft as a part of the International Space Station Expeditions 59, 60 and 61. Koch, who had worked as a research associate in the United States Antarctic Program between 2004 and 2007, is currently the only person alive to have both wintered at the South Pole and been a crew member at the International Space Station.

89

WEATHER BALLOON

Since the late 19th century, weather balloons have become a workhorse of meteorological and atmospheric observations. Mostly made from highly flexible latex and filled with hydrogen or helium, modern weather balloons can expand close to 200 times their original volume as they ascend to altitudes of up to 40km (25 miles), carrying instruments to record atmospheric pressure, temperature, humidity and wind speed.

Twice a day, 365 days a year, weather balloons are released from 900 locations worldwide to collect the necessary data for local weather forecasting, and to provide and share the long-term data sets necessary for scientists to better understand the global climate. First initiated some 60 years ago and now managed by the United Nations' World Meteorological Organisation, this effort represents one of the most successful instances of international scientific collaboration.

With fewer than 50 permanent research stations scattered across a land mass nearly twice the size of Australia, Antarctica continues to present huge challenges for meteorological and atmospheric observation, especially in its inland regions. Even with the increase in satellite monitoring of the Earth's atmosphere, direct measurements remain crucial to achieve local precision. But because weather balloons need to be launched manually, a wide disparity exists between the density of data that can be collected in populated and under-populated regions of the world. The majority of launch locations are in the northern hemisphere. Antarctica has the fewest.

Weather balloons were first deployed and tested in the Antarctic by French, British and German expeditions during the first two decades of the 20th century. In 1909, Jean-Baptiste Charcot attached a message to a balloon 'without a hope

New Zealand postage stamp depicting meteorological research at Scott Base, 1984. © NZ Post, New Zealand

that it should ever be retrieved' by anyone who might be able to help to retrace its trajectory. By the time of Robert Falcon Scott's 1910–13 *Terra Nova* expedition, however, a technique had been introduced whereby a silk thread was attached to a little temperature and pressure recorder carried under the balloon. The thread unrolled as the balloon ascended, until, at a given altitude of no more than 8km (5 miles), the device detached itself and came down beneath a small parachute. Once on the ground, it could be retrieved by following the thread from the launch site.

Retrieving data was made easier from the 1930s onwards with the introduction of radios that could

Scientist launching a weather balloon at Japan's Showa Station, 2020. © Getty Images/Kyodo News

transmit data directly back to base. Today, weather balloons can also be tracked by satellite positioning systems and are equipped with sophisticated radiosondes able to take measurements every two seconds, then to relay them across hundreds of kilometres. Parachutes are still used to carry the radiosondes back to the ground.

Recent but transitory efforts to increase the volume of weather and atmospheric data in Antarctica have included the 2018–19 International Year of Polar Prediction, which saw the launch of an additional 2,200 weather balloons across the continent over a three-month period. This co-ordinated effort not only improved the prediction of storms and cyclones in Antarctica, but has also confirmed that the lower atmosphere has been warming over the last 30 years.

90

SWIMSUIT

The Southern Ocean harbours some of the coldest water temperatures on Earth. South of the Antarctic Convergence, the temperature of seawater can drop as low as nearly -2°C (28°F), thus remaining liquid below freezing point as a result of its salt content.

Much research has gone into protective gear to allow humans to swim in these waters in order to collect specimens and research marine biodiversity. During Operation *Highjump* in 1946–47, the United States Navy tested early examples of cold water swimsuits in the ice-laden water of the Bay of Whales. The suits consisted of a sealed one-piece outer layer made of rubber. Wearing

United States Navy testing cold water immersion suits in the Bay of Whales, 1946. © United States Navy. Courtesy of the United States Antarctic Program Photo Library, United States.

just a pair of long underwear underneath, the swimmers managed to stay in the water for around 20 minutes without any harmful effects.

Nowadays, Antarctic divers sometimes rely on hot water suits or dry suits to protect them from the ice-cold water. Dry suits allow divers more autonomy than hot water suits, which require the diver to be linked to a boat via an umbilical cord through which hot water is pumped down and circulated around the diver's body.

The availability of this ever improving technology, however, does not discourage some intrepid souls from diving into Antarctic waters wearing only swimsuits – or in some cases nothing at all. While the most obvious illustration of this is the tourists who take part in what is known as the polar plunge during Antarctic cruises, the most remarkable example is the growing trend in record-breaking Antarctic swims.

In 2002, with the express intention of testing the limits of human endurance, American swimmer Lynne Cox was the first person to carry out a long-distance swim in the Antarctic. She swam 1.96km (1.2 miles), spending 25 minutes in water at 0°C (32°F). Since this had never been done, Cox was unsure about coming out of the water alive. She described the water as viscous, like cooled-down engine oil. While the hardest thing during her swim was to keep breathing. It also took months for the sensation in her fingers and

Lewis Pugh's swimsuit, cap and goggles, an example of 'Speedo diplomacy', 2020. © Courtesy of Lewis Pugh

toes to fully return. Cox still holds the record for having swum the furthest distance in Antarctica wearing just a swimsuit.

The record for the most southerly swim is held by the Israeli-born South African Ram Barkai, who in 2008 completed a 1km (0.62 mile) swim in one of Antarctica's rare open lakes, Long Lake, near India's Maitri research station. Perhaps the best-known Antarctic swimmer is the British-South African Lewis Pugh, who has completed several Antarctic swims.

In 2020 Pugh became the first person to swim along a river of surface melt water on the edges of the East Antarctic ice sheet. As a 'United Nations Patron of the Oceans', Pugh uses his swims to draw attention to the vulnerability of marine ecosystems around the world. In 2016, he was instrumental in securing the international agreement to establish a Marine Protected Area (MPA) in the Ross Sea, and he continues to campaign for other MPAs in the Weddell Sea and around East Antarctica. Pugh's swims and campaigning achievements have been described as 'Speedo diplomacy'.

91

TIDE GAUGE

As early as the 1957–58 International Geophysical Year, it was common knowledge within the scientific community that glaciers were experiencing unprecedented melt worldwide. The reason, however, was still unknown.

In a 1957 BBC broadcast, *The Restless Sphere*, introducing the International Geophysical Year to the British public, the Duke of Edinburgh explained that 'glaciers are being studied, partly because they make up ten per cent of the world's land surface, but principally, because they're melting away. And the sea level is rising at the rate of two and a half inches a century. If they melted away altogether, seaport cities of the world, like London and New York, would be completely submerged, as the level of the sea would rise over a hundred feet.' In 1959, Laurence Kirwan, the secretary of the Royal Geographical Society, wrote: 'both Arctic and Antarctic, it seems, are slowly melting, almost imperceptibly changing, for their ice cover is melting and adding minutely to the volume of the oceans.'

Sea level rise is now understood to be caused by two factors resulting from anthropogenic climate change. Water is added to the oceans by glacial melt, and oceans

Inspecting the upgrade work conducted at the Port Vila tide station, Vanuatu. © Pacific Community (SPC)/Vanuatu

gain in volume through thermal expansion as they become warmer.

According to the United States' National Oceanographic and Atmospheric Administration, global sea levels have already risen about 21–24cm (8.3–9.4in) since the rapid global industrialisation of the late 19th century, and at a drastically accelerated rate since the start of the 21st century. Rising sea levels have led to increased coastal flooding, threats to local infrastructure, stress on coastal ecosystems, and even deadlier and more severe storms. A growing number of locations around the world are becoming uninhabitable, leading to the growth of climate refugees.

Many of those affected by this sea level rise are among the most marginalised communities in the world; people who have low carbon footprints and lack the resources to relocate as their homelands vanish underwater. Small island

nations, notably Tuvalu, the Maldives, Kiribati, Vanuatu and the Marshall Islands, have already lost significant territory.

Tide gauges – instruments that make systematic sea level observations – have been used in coastal areas such as Amsterdam and London since the 17th century to measure tidal surges and determine tidal patterns. Their continuous and consistent recordings over the last few centuries have allowed scientists to see real changes in the tide levels, changes that would be impossible to track if we did not have these historical recordings as a baseline.

This tide gauge, located at Port Vila on the coast of the Republic of Vanuatu, measures the rising waters in the region. Unless drastic changes are made in global climate policy, the melting of Antarctic glaciers will make Vanuatu uninhabitable within a century.

A man sits on a protective sandbag wall defending Guraidhoo, an island in the Maldives, against sea level rise. © Getty Images/Allison Joyce/Stringer

92

WEDDING DRESS

Antarctica has had its share of deaths and even births. In recent years, it has also become an increasingly popular location for weddings. In 2017, polar guides Julie Baum and Tom Sylvester celebrated the first wedding to be held in a sector of Antarctica claimed by the United Kingdom. The wedding, held at Rothera Station on Adelaide Island, was performed by station leader Paul Samways, sworn in as a magistrate for the British Antarctic Territory for the occasion.

Baum and Sylvester, who were hired to manage deep field science expeditions by the British Antarctic Survey in 2016, had been together for eleven years and engaged for three. 'We've been through all sorts of adventures together,' said Sylvester days before the ceremony. 'In fact we haven't really left each other's sides for the past ten years ... It's just been the best time of my life.' According to Baum, 'Getting married in Antarctica feels like it was meant to be. There is no better place really.'

Eric Bourne and Stephen Carpenter's wedding on the RSS *Sir David Attenborough*, 2022. © Rich Turner, British Antarctic Survey, Cambridge, United Kingdom

Having decided to get married in Rothera, Sylvester made brass wedding rings in the station's metal workshop. Baum and her friends made her wedding dress, using part of an orange pyramid tent as her 'something old'.

On 15 July 2017, they began their wedding day with a champagne breakfast. The ceremony took place in a specially designed chapel made from bed sheets. Although their families were absent, the wedding was attended by their fellow overwinterers, posing outdoors for photos in -9°C (15.8°F). Afterwards, the party enjoyed three wedding cakes prepared by Rothera's resident chef. The couple then 'departed' in their wedding vehicle, a Sno-Cat.

Five years later, on 24 April 2022, Stephen Carpenter and Eric Bourne, stewards on the RRS *Sir David Attenborough* icebreaker, wed on the ship's helideck in the first same-sex marriage to take place in the British Antarctic Territory.

Just like Antarctic births, there are geopolitical implications to Antarctic marriages. The British government allows any couple who can legally marry in England or Wales to also apply for a licence through the British Antarctic Territory Administration. But they do caution that 'under the Antarctic Treaty, the UK does not seek to assert its sovereignty against other Treaty Parties'.

Julie Baum and Tom Sylvester's wedding at Rothera Station, 2017. Photo by Blair Fyffe. © Julie Baum

Therefore, any marriage between British citizens is valid within the UK, but other citizens must have their marriages validated elsewhere.

According to the British Antarctic Survey, stories like this prove 'that it's never too cold for true love'.

93

MICROPLASTIC

Microplastics, fragments of plastic less than 5mm (0.2in) in length, have become a global environmental menace. Virtually all plastic ever created still exists. Sooner or later, much of it ends up in our water and makes its way into the ocean.

The sources of microplastics are varied. One common source are the tiny pieces used in air blasting technology, or in exfoliating hand and face wash, which are manufactured to wash down the drain. The other main source comes from larger plastics that deteriorate into increasingly small pieces, or from water used to wash synthetic clothing, carrying their fibres into the sea. Eventually finding their way into the ocean, microplastics settle into the marine environment, are eaten by fish, and remain as a physical contaminant.

Due to the interrelated nature of the global ocean, as well as the long history of humans bringing plastics to the region, microplastics have already reached Antarctica. In 2020, a team of British scientists published results showing at least one particle of microplastic for every gram of sediment in the Antarctic seabed, similar to the rate of microplastic pollution in the most populated regions of the world.

Microplastics have also made their way beyond the surface water and sediments, and are now present in Antarctic ice. In 2020, an Australian study of sea ice samples gathered in East Antarctica revealed the presence of 14 types of plastic fragments. Microplastics have even infiltrated the Antarctic food chain. As early as 1988, Dutch researchers discovered plastic fragments in the stomach contents of petrels breeding in Antarctica. In 2003, an

Australian team discovered microplastics in fur seal excrement on the subantarctic Macquarie Island. In 2019, a team largely consisting of Portuguese scientists demonstrated the presence of microplastics in the excrement of gentoo penguins. And in 2020, an Italian research team on King George Island showed that microplastics are present in the guts of Antarctic springtails, which feed primarily on moss and lichen.

The 21st century has seen the global community becoming more protective of Antarctic environments than ever before, but it has also revealed that human devastation to the fragile Antarctic regions has been greater than was previously ever imagined.

Disintegration of a plastic bottle into microplastic. © Getty Images/ImaZinS

Scientists collecting water and sediment samples for microplastic analysis, Larsemann Hills, East Antarctica, 2020. © Courtesy of Cheryl A Noronha-D'Mello, National Centre for Polar and Ocean Research, Ministry of Earth Sciences, Goa, India

94

DOUGLAS DC-3

Ever since pioneering aviators Richard Byrd, Hubert Wilkins and Hjalmar Riiser-Larsen first took to the skies above Antarctica in the late 1920s, aircraft have occupied a central role in Antarctic exploration and logistics. Not only did their introduction enable explorers to chart in just a few hours regions that previously took months to explore, but planes and helicopters also went on to facilitate the safe and speedy deployment of goods and personnel. In this, they have proved valuable assets not only for Antarctic science, but also for taking geopolitical advantage, where the ability to support remote stations and field camps translates into influence in governance.

When it comes to aerial dominance for scientific and strategic advantage, no nation comes close to the United States, whose Antarctic Program operates more than a dozen aircraft. This fleet includes six Hercules LC-130s operated by the Air National Guard, each with a payload of 20 tons and mostly used for resupplying the South Pole Station; and a US Air Force C-17 Globemaster able to transport 55 tons and mostly used between New Zealand and McMurdo Station.

Ski-equipped Hercules LC-130 operated by the United States Air National Guard for the United States Antarctic Program, 2018. Photo by Mike Lucibella. © National Science Foundation. Courtesy of United States Antarctic Program Photo Library, United States

Particularly important strategically in supporting a growing number of American deep field camps are the LC-130s, the largest ski-equipped aircraft in the world, produced by Lockheed and only available to the United States.

Other Antarctic programmes that operate continental or intercontinental aircraft to and within Antarctica are Chile, Argentina, the United Kingdom, New Zealand, Australia, Russia and China. There are also a number of private operators that transport adventure tourists to Antarctica from Chile and South Africa, as well as operating flights within the continent.

Key to establishing intercontinental air bridges with Antarctica are airstrips, which are not only expensive but also technically complicated to maintain, especially on ice. Despite the costs, however, the current trend is for the ongoing expansion of air capability in Antarctica, with several nations currently investing in new aircraft and airstrips. For example, Australia, which began by leasing a commercial Airbus passenger plane to carry personnel to Antarctica, has recently scaled up by landing a C-17 at its new Wilkins airstrip. Italy has recently built a gravel airstrip able to receive Hercules, Airbus and C-17 aircraft near its Zucchelli Station, and the United States

Snow Eagle 601, a Douglas DC-3 operated by the Chinese National Antarctic Research Program, 2019. © CHINARE, Shanghai, China

too is planning a hard ice airstrip at the South Pole on which to land its C-17s.

Further exemplifying the strategic importance of aerial capacity in Antarctica is China's acquisition of its first aircraft, as well as its plans for an ice airstrip able to receive larger intercontinental aircraft. Named *Snow Eagle 601*, this ski-equipped Douglas DC-3 was entirely refitted by Basler Turbo from the airframe of a 1940 aircraft that flew over Normandy on D-Day. One among a number of the versatile DC-3s utilised in Antarctica, *Snow Eagle* is fitted with instruments such as ice-penetrating radar and gravimeters, and transports supplies and personnel to China's deep field camps, including to its Kunlun Station at Dome A, the highest point of the Antarctic ice sheet. *Snow Eagle 601* personifies China's rapidly expanding Antarctic programme, as well as its long-term ambitions on the continent.

95

AUTONOMOUS UNDERWATER VEHICLE

First pioneered in the Arctic in 1996, Autonomous Underwater Vehicles (AUVs) have been successfully deployed in Antarctica since 2001. In contrast to Remotely Operated Underwater Vehicles (ROVs), which are linked to the surface by an umbilical cable to power the vehicle and transmit commands and information, AUVs are autonomous submersible robots commanded from the surface via radio signals, and with a battery-powered autonomy that can extend to 100 hours.

Often resembling torpedoes, the largest AUVs can measure more than 6m (19.7ft), dive to depths of 6,000m (19,685ft), and carry multiple instruments. In what has become an increasingly competitive commercial and technological field with Swedish, German, Australian, American and other international companies vying for dominance, new types of AUVs are currently rolled out almost every year, with improved capabilities in terms of range, manoeuvrability and data collection.

In recent years, despite their cost, which runs into millions of dollars, AUVs have become increasingly indispensable tools for oceanographic and glaciological research in Antarctica

and have already contributed massively to our understanding of the continent and its surrounding ocean. They are now used for everything from mapping the seafloor and its biodiversity to monitoring the variability of sea ice thickness, studying the ocean-sea ice interface, and collecting data on previously unexplored marine environments.

Indeed, among the most urgent research for which AUVs are currently being used is the study of marine environments beneath the Larsen ice shelves on the eastern side of the Antarctic Peninsula, and the Thwaites Glacier in the Bellingshausen Sea sector of West Antarctica. Ice shelves are floating extensions of the Antarctic ice sheet that is itself grounded on the continent. Ice shelves buttress the ice sheet from which they derive by slowing down their flow from land to sea. Because they are floating, however, ice shelves are particularly vulnerable to melting from beneath as water temperatures warm in the Southern Ocean.

Both the Larsen A and Larsen B ice shelves have suffered catastrophic losses over the past quarter century, and A-68, an iceberg about 100 times the size of Manhattan, calved off Larsen C in 2017. Meanwhile, the Thwaites Glacier and its neighbouring Pine Island Glacier have doubled their rate of ice loss over the past 30 years. About the size of Florida, the Thwaites Glacier holds enough ice to raise global sea levels by 65cm (26in) if it were to collapse entirely, and could unleash an added 1–3.5m (3.3–11.5ft) of sea level rise by draining the West Antarctic Ice Sheet that it currently helps to buttress.

Faced with the urgent need to monitor and predict the response of the Thwaites Glacier to global warming and the potentially devastating consequences for coastal communities and habitats around the world, the International Thwaites Glacier Collaboration is co-ordinating the work of scientists from Europe and the United States with AUVs as their most prominent tool. With AUVs, it can be said that robots have never been more important in helping humanity come to grips with its biggest self-inflicted challenges.

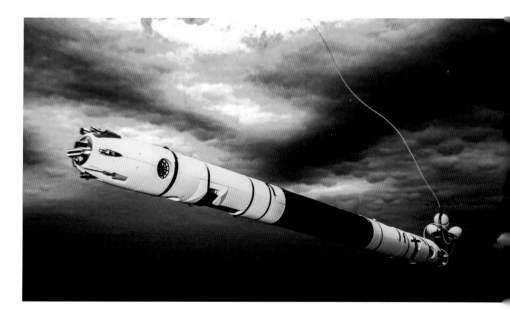

'Boaty McBoatface'. Autonomous Underwater Vehicle (AUV), named following a public poll, and used to study the Thwaites Glacier, 2017. Named following a public poll. © Courtesy of the British National Oceanography Centre, Southampton, United Kingdom

'Icefin'. Remotely Operated Underwater Vehicle (ROV) operating beneath Antarctic sea ice. Photo by Rob Robbins. © Courtesy of Britney Schmidt, Cornell University, Ithaca, United States

96

D-AIR LAB ANTARCTIC SUIT

Clothing choices and efficiency have proved to be defining factors in the success and failure of Antarctic expeditions.

In the early days of the continent's exploration, Roald Amundsen's strategy of combining traditional and modern techniques and materials was the most successful approach: 'In undertaking a sledge journey down there in autumn or spring, the most extraordinary precautions have to be taken to protect oneself against the cold. [Reindeer] skin clothing is then the only thing that is of any use; but at this time of year ... one can go for a long time without being more heavily clad than a lumberman working in the woods. During the march our clothing was usually the following: two sets of woollen underclothes, of which that nearest the skin was quite thin. Outside the shirt we wore either an ordinary waistcoat or a comparatively light knitted woollen jersey. Outside all came our excellent Burberry clothes — trousers and jacket.'

The animal-skin clothing used in extremely cold conditions was inspired by the Netsilik Inuit encountered by Amundsen during his first transit of the Northwest Passage. This clothing provided insulation by trapping a layer of air that was warmed by the body and avoided sweating by allowing the air to circulate.

Today, the most widely used modern Antarctic clothing is the United States Antarctic Program's Extreme Cold Weather (ECW) gear. The ECW comprises some 30 items, ranging from the iconic red parka to eight pairs of gloves and mittens for different conditions. The ECW echoes the benefits of Amundsen's multi-layered approach, which has become the norm in polar and mountaineering clothing but also presents limitations in terms of weight.

This is why the non-profit agency for change UNLESS invited D-Air Lab to develop solutions to lighten polar clothing and make it less cumbersome. Specialising in textile innovation and the protection of the human body through the application of airbag technology to clothing, the innovative Italian start-up D-Air Lab has set out to design an intelligent Antarctic suit that combines 'advanced wearable technologies and the intelligence of analogue handcrafting experience' to manufacture what UNLESS refers to as a 'first architectural envelope'.

Tested in 2019 at the Franco-Italian station Concordia, the first prototype of the D-Air Lab Antarctic suit comprises an inner and an outer component and is intended to keep scientists warm when working in temperatures as low as -50°C (-58°F). Worn against the skin, the inner suit incorporates silver thread to create conductive paths to generate heat and a system of 'tunnels' to provide airflow and regulate moisture. These are controlled by an electronic system that processes the information retrieved from sensors around the body, monitoring temperature and vital bodily functions in order to redistribute warmth intelligently – but not so differently from Netsilik reindeer-skin clothing. The outer suit provides advanced protection against the elements and works as a lightweight 'armour' impermeable to the wind and drift snow.

Inner and outer envelopes of the Antarctic suit by UNLESS and D-Air Lab, 2021. © D-Air Lab, Milan, Italy

97

SHIPWRECK

Weddell Sea, 21 November 1915: 'This evening, as we were lying in our tents we heard the Boss call out, "She's going, boys!"... She went down bows first, her stern raised in the air. She then gave one quick dive and the ice closed over her for ever.'

Little did Ernest Shackleton imagine that 107 years later, a private expedition equipped with a powerful steel icebreaker and Automated Underwater Vehicles would succeed in locating the wooden wreck of the *Endurance* lying at a depth of 3,008m (6,588ft). Not only did the South African icebreaker *Agulhas II* have to navigate the same unpredictable pack ice that

had crushed the *Endurance*, but the documented co-ordinates of her sinking were themselves an approximation. On the day she sank, the sky was overcast and her captain, Frank Worsley, was unable to fix her position using astronomical observations. Instead, he relied on 'dead reckoning', and a reading made the previous day, to estimate as best he could how far and in what

direction the ship had drifted in the ice flow by the time it went down.

Based on marine archaeologist Mensun Bound's interpretation of these co-ordinates, the shipwreck was eventually discovered just 7km (4.3 miles) from Worsley's estimation, the ghostly figure of the *Endurance* emerged eerily preserved by the 0.1°C (32.2°F) water temperatures and the absence of wood-eating worms at the bottom of the Weddell Sea.

Originally commissioned by Adrien de Gerlache and Lars Christensen as a luxury yacht for Arctic hunting parties, she was purchased by Shackleton in 1914. Her wreckage was designated a Historic Site by the Antarctic Treaty System in 2019, the same year as Bound's first failed attempt at finding her. Forbidden from touching any part of it, the *Endurance22* expedition documented the wreck site using video and high-resolution 3D radar.

In a region that has been the stage for so many stories of courage, heroism and fortitude, the story of the *Endurance* remains the most popular tale of an Antarctic adventure, often labelled as the 'greatest survival story of all time'. Our collective fascination and even nostalgia Shackleton's *Endurance* expedition is demonstrated by the countless books and museum exhibitions revisiting the subject from numerous angles, including celebrations of Frank Hurley's photographs, lessons that CEOs can take from Shackleton's leadership, and a children's novel written from the perspective of the ship's cat, Mrs Chippy.

This fascination with the *Endurance* story, and the Heroic Age more generally, has led to a buoyant

Members of the 2013 Shackleton Epic Expedition, their replica of the *James Caird* in the background, moments after landing on South Georgia. © Shackleton Epic Expedition, 2013

market in period artefacts, with increasingly high prices achieved at auction, as well as much cheaper replicas available at museum gift shops. It has also resulted in a growing number of people undertaking re-enactments of portions of this, and other, expeditions in order to experience them first hand. A handful of adventure tourism companies, for example, offer 'in the footsteps' expeditions to re-enact Shackleton's 30 hour crossing of South Georgia from King Haakon Bay to Stromness. More extreme was Australian adventurer Tim Jarvis' 2007 re-enactment of Shackleton's journey from Elephant Island to South Georgia. For this re-enactment, Jarvis and his five companions built an exact replica of the *James Caird* and used the same materials, clothing, instruments and food that Shackleton and his men had employed in 1916.

Nothing, however, beats the search for and discovery of the wreck of the *Endurance,* which Shackleton himself believed was lost forever, as a manifestation of the Heroic Age's enduring grip on our collective imagination.

The wreck of the Endurance, discovered at a depth of 3,008m (6,588ft) in the Weddell Sea on 5 March 2022. © Falklands Maritime Heritage Trust/National Geographic

98

TROWEL

While the Heroic Age expeditions of Ernest Shackleton and Robert Falcon Scott continue to garner a great deal of public attention, many Antarctic stories remain unknown. Through the dedicated and careful work of a growing number of archaeologists visiting the region each year, we continue to learn about the long interactions between humans and the Antarctic environment.

Not only are archaeologists becoming more numerous in Antarctica, but heritage has become an increasingly important component of many Antarctic programmes. A number of countries also have museums that specifically highlight their national contributions to Antarctic exploration and science. Some, like New Zealand and the United Kingdom, have heritage trusts with the stated purpose of saving and preserving historic sites within their territorial claims. The geopolitical significance of Antarctic heritage was possibly at the heart of an archaeological mystery in 1975, when stone arrowheads were recovered from Chilean bottom-sampling operations of King George Island. Rather than indicating undocumented expeditions by Terra del Fuegans, these artifacts turned out to have been planted, perhaps as a joke, or perhaps in an effort to strengthen territorial claims.

Concerns over preserving human history in Antarctica extend beyond national boundaries. For example, in 2001, the International Committee for Polar Heritage was established with the primary goal of promoting 'international co-operation in the protection and conservation of non-Indigenous heritage in the Arctic and Antarctic'. Under the Antarctic Treaty System, Historic Sites and Monuments (HSMs) are one of three types of protected areas, currently covering approximately one hundred sites throughout the Antarctic region.

Trowel used by archaeologist Andres Zarankin in over 15 Antarctic excavations since 1995. © Andrés Zarankin, Universidade Federal de Minas Gerais, Belo Horizonte, Brazil

Archaeological dig at Byers Peninsula, Livingston Island, in 2017. © Andrés Zarankin, Universidade Federal de Minas Gerais, Belo Horizonte, Brazil

While today's Antarctic visitors document every aspect of their experiences, archaeologists seek to discover those who did not have the means of documenting and sharing their experiences. The most evocative discoveries by Antarctic archaeologists are those that date back to a time when the life of sealers inhabiting its desolate outlying islands was rudimentary in the extreme.

Among these, perhaps the most poignant is a mestizo woman's skeletal remains, including her skull, dating from the early 1820s and discovered by Chilean scientist Daniel Torres on Livingstone Island in 1985. While the reasons for this woman's presence at a sealing beach camp so early in Antarctic history remains unknown, hypotheses have often pointed towards exploitation. Whatever the truth, her remains indicate that women arrived in the Antarctic region far earlier than is often cited. They also remind us of all the working-class and racially diverse crews of whaling, sailing and naval vessels who left few traces of their presence but were nonetheless

Antarctic explorers, venturing into the unknown with little chance of success.

Because Antarctic journeys require enormous support, the numbers of these unnamed visitors increased with time, ranging from enlisted naval personnel to the supporting staff at research stations, whose work in carpentry, mechanics or dishwashing is essential, but receives little public recognition. Cruise ship operations are reliant on countless crew members and hotel staff, most often from Southeast Asia, who return to Antarctica year on year and are among the record holders for the number of visits to Antarctica across the Drake Passage.

As archaeologists piece together evidence to reconstruct the lives of unrecognised people in Antarctic history, perhaps we should expand our own definitions of what constitutes Antarctic explorers and remember that Antarctic exploration, science and tourism are dependent on veritable armies of less visible workers.

99

NOTEBOOK

A blank page, especially if it is the first of an empty notebook, is both an invitation and a challenge. In its vacuity, it also echoes Antarctica's denuded interior: the whiteness that distinguishes the continent on the world map.

Notebook. © Getty Images/Flavio Coelho

Even as new technologies have come to dominate Antarctica, many visitors still rely on the oldest: a pencil and a notebook. Whether they are scientific or personal, writing down observations – to temporarily hold ideas until they can be better organised and transcribed – is an extremely powerful act. For some, the use of a notebook is motivated by the desire to share with others, or by the possible professional and reputational gain derived from publishing their results and adventures. For others, it is a more private enterprise, motivated by the need to make sense of the space, or to revisit feelings and emotions.

Despite its frequent symbolic representation as a blank page – or blank canvas – Antarctica's primordial desolation and minerality can often overwhelm the senses. In fact, according to the historian Stephen Pyne, the great ice sheet that covers much of the continent can overpower language itself: 'This is geography encroaching on nihilism. Ice covers Earth and saturates the sky. Everything the ice touches it reduces … There is no shape, no perspective, no colour, no movement, no objects, no inherent contrasts. The scene is meaningful only by comparison to other scenes, comparisons that always seem to end in negation: The ice absorbs, it does not emanate. It challenges not only visual arts but literature. Language is pared to mono syllables, stripped of descriptive complexity … ice … sky … cloud … sun … blue … white … moon … cold…'

On the other hand, like the blank pages of a notebook, the perceived blankness of the Antarctic landscape can serve as a perfect backdrop upon which to project and express the full breadth of our human imagination. American science-fiction writer Ursula K Le

Aerial photograph of the East Antarctic ice sheet taken for by the United States Geological Survey for cartographic purposes, 1961. © United States Geological Survey, Virginia, United States

Guin's 1982 short story 'Sur', for example, tells the tale of a group of nine Chilean, Argentine and Peruvian women who undertake a secret expedition to Antarctica in 1909. During this expedition, they march across the polar plateau and become the first to reach the South Pole. As they turn back home, however, they wipe away their footprints and leave nothing behind to mark their achievement, preferring instead to leave the landscape blank for later explorers to experience and claim as if they were the first.

The blank page of a notebook thus takes on practical significance as an enduring object for 'Antarcticans' to record their thoughts and observations, but also serves as a metaphysical representation of the idea of Antarctica as a still largely untrodden realm, open for new stories to be written on to and from within.

100

PIER

It is often said that the Antarctic continent is something of 'another world': one whose environmental inhospitality, absence of native population or proprietor, exotic fauna, and nearly complete lack of vegetation makes it a land apart; characterised less by its similarities than by its differences with other continents. Although more than 4,000 seasonal workers migrate to Antarctica every year, it remains impossible to settle or to survive there without external support. A visit to Antarctica, whether it is motivated by science, adventure, contemplation or simply money, is never open-ended. The only possibility is to visit and – if the journey does not prove fatal – to return.

Historically, the points of departure and return to and from Antarctica have consisted of piers and runways in what have since been called 'Antarctic gateways'; those ports and cities lying closest to the Southern Ocean and Antarctica. They include Lyttelton, Christchurch and Invercargill on New Zealand's South Island; Hobart and Fremantle in Australia; Cape Town in South Africa; Ushuaia in Argentina; Punta Arenas in Chile; the island of South Georgia, and the Falkland Islands (Malvinas). While New Zealand and Australia were once the start and end points to some of the most famous episodes in Antarctic history and remain logistical hubs for many of the largest national Antarctic programmes, no pier has marked the beginnings and endings of more Antarctic journeys than the one at Ushuaia.

Located along the Beagle Channel in Tierra del Fuego, often branded as the *fin del mondo* (the 'end of the world'), Ushuaia is the southernmost city in the world, and the closest to the Antarctic continent, about two days' sailing across the Drake Passage. Despite also being home to the Admiral Berisso Naval Base, which supports Argentina's Antarctic programme and logistics, Ushuaia has become better known as the point of embarkation for the tens of thousands of Antarctic pilgrims who board cruise ships to

Antarctica every austral summer. Indeed, since its beginnings in the 1960s, Antarctic tourism has become a major industry and contributor to Ushuaia's local economy, one that is envied by neighbouring Chile, which has thus far only managed to seize a much smaller portion of this growing tourism market.

Far from such economic concerns, however, for those privileged enough to travel to the *fin del Mundo*, embark on an Antarctic-bound vessel and return some ten days later, the pier at Ushuaia is something of a revolving door through which one comes full circle, leaving behind and then returning to the cacophony of civilisation. In between extends what many experience and describe as the quintessence of wilderness, the natural world's most majestic and elevating preserve. Like seeing the curvature of the Earth from space and experiencing weightlessness, then crashing back down to Earth in a capsule, a journey to Antarctica, to and from the pier at Ushuaia, rarely leaves visitors indifferent – or untouched.

And yet, with every new visitor, Antarctica becomes a little more accessible, a little more humanised, a little less 'other'.

The pier in Ushuaia. © Getty Images/Yinwei Liu

Antarctic cruise ships docked in the port of Ushuaia, the capital of Tierra del Fuego, Argentina.
© Getty Images/Wolfgang Kaehler/LightRocket

CONCLUSION

Antarctica is not one thing.

As this book shows, the Antarctic is a kaleidoscope; an assembly of environments, habitats, nations, people, technologies, and ideas. Antarctica, its surrounding seas and islands, mean different things to different people, depending on their perspective and context.

As much as we tried to be inclusive, writing this book was a reminder of our own blindspots and ignorance. While we are a man and a woman, a European and an American, a Generation X and a Millennial, we have similar educational backgrounds and areas of expertise regarding Antarctic history. How different might our selection of objects have been if one of us were a scientist, or hailed from the Global South, or were a generation older or younger?

One of the satisfactions derived from selecting our 100 objects was indeed being challenged to think differently about the many historical facets and dimensions that have gone into shaping our different perceptions and experiences of Antarctica; from the global to the personal, from the geopolitical to the intimate and from the physical to the intellectual. One of the frustrations, of course, is that the approach also required us to leave out some important objects and stories.

While in our text we highlighted notable contributions to Antarctic science and exploration from around the world, it is a fact that the majority of stories in these pages are dominated by Europeans and Americans – mostly white and mostly men. This is, to an extent, a reflection of Antarctic history. Growing communities of Antarcticans, however, are seeking to change that, and advocate for better inclusion for those who have been historically excluded.

We hope that the wide community of polar enthusiasts have appreciated our take on the material history of Antarctica, and those new to Antarctic history are inspired to learn more. Although Neil MacGregor's *A History of the World in 100 Objects*, published in 2010, has sparked something of a trend and seen its recipe become a formula, as film director Alfred Hitchcock once said: 'It is better to start with a cliché than to end with one'. Indeed, one of our specific aims has been to break some of the clichés that often constrain Antarctic history.

Supplies and Homes Building Up at Little America, by Robert Charles Haun, 1956.© Courtesy of the United States Navy History and Heritage Command, Washington DC, United States

100 ANTARCTIC BOOKS

Reflecting the contents of this book, the list below is by definition selective. Its aim is to provide a broad historical, geographical and thematic cross section of some of the books available for those wishing to read more about Antarctic history. Many have informed our own work, and in some cases have been directly quoted from in order to enrich our texts with Antarctic voices.

FIRST-HAND ACCOUNTS AND MEMOIRS

Amundsen, Roald, *The South Pole: An Account of the Norwegian Antarctic Expedition in the* Fram, *1910–12* (New York, N.Y: Cooper Square Press, 2000).

Arnesen, Liv and Bancroft, Ann with Dahle, Cheryl, *No Horizon Is So Far: Two Women and Their Historic Journey across Antarctica* (Minneapolis: University of Minnesota Press, 2019).

Aston, Felicity, *Call of the White: Taking the World to the South Pole* (Chichester: Summersdale Publishers, 2012).

Borchgrevink, CE, *First on the Antarctic Continent: Being an Account of the British Antarctic Expedition, 1898–1900* (Cambridge: University of Cambridge Press, 2014).

Bull, Henrik Johan, *The Cruise of the 'Antarctic' to the South Polar Regions* (London: Edward Arnold, 1896).

Byrd, Richard E, *Alone: The Classic Polar Adventure* (Washington, DC: Island Press, 2003).

Charcot, Jean-Baptiste, *Le Français au Pôle Sud / Le Pourquoi-Pas? dans l'Antarctique* (Paris: Arthaud, 2013).

Cherry-Garrard, Apsley, *The Worst Journey in the World* (New York: Penguin Classics, 2006).

Cook, Frederick A, *Through the First Antarctic Night* (London: William Heinemann, 1900).

Cook, James, *A voyage towards the South Pole and round the world. Performed in His Majesty's ships the Resolution and Adventure, in the years 1772, 1773, 1774, and 1775. Written by James Cook, commander of the Resolution. In which is included, Captain Furneaux's Narrative of his Proceedings in the Adventure during the Separation of the Ships.*

In two volumes. Illustrated with Maps and Charts, and a Variety of Portraits of Persons and Views of Places, drawn during the Voyage by Mr. Hodges, and engraved by the most eminent Masters (London: Printed for W. Strahan, 1784).

Dalrymple, Alexander, *An historical collection of the several voyages and discoveries in the South Pacific Ocean* (Cambridge: University of Cambridge Press, 2015).

Darlington, Jennie, *My Antarctic Honeymoon: A Year At The Bottom of the World* (New York: Doubleday & Co., 1956).

Dewart, Gilbert, *Antarctic Comrades: An American With the Russians in Antarctica* (Columbus: Ohio State University Press, 1989).

Dufek, George J, *Operation Deepfreeze* (New York: Harcourt, Brace, 1957).

Fiennes, Ranulph, *To the Ends of the Earth* (New York: Simon & Schuster Ltd, 2014).

Fuchs, Vivian and Hillary, Edmund, *The Crossing of Antarctica: The Commonwealth Trans-Antarctic Expedition 1955–8* (London: Cassell & Company Limited, 1958).

Giaever, John, *The White Desert: The Official Account of the Norwegian-British-Swedish Antarctic Expedition* (London: Chatto & Windus, 1954).

Hardy, Alister, *Great Waters: A Voyage of Natural History to Study Whales, Plankton and the Waters of the Southern Ocean* (New York: Harper & Row, 1967).

Hillary, Edmund, *No Latitude for Error* (London: Hodder & Stoughton, 1961).

Hooper, Meredith, *The Ferocious Summer: Palmer's Penguins and the Warming of Antarctica* (London: Profile Books Ltd, 2007).

Johnson, Nicholas, *Big Dead Place: Inside the Strange & Menacing World of Antarctica* (Los Angeles: Feral House, 2005).

Liotard, André-Frank and Pommier, Robert, *Terre Adélie* (Paris: Arthaud, 1952).

Mawson, Douglas, *The Home of the Blizzard: An Australian Hero's Classic Tale of Antarctic Discovery and Adventure* (Cambridge, Massachusetts: Wakefield Press, 2010).

Messner, Reinhold, *Antarctica: Both Heaven and Hell* (Marlborough, Wiltshire: The Crowood Press Ltd, 1991).

Murphy, Robert Cushman, *Logbook for Grace: Whaling brig Daisy, 1912–13* (New York: Time Incorporated, 1965).

Nielsen, Jerri, *Ice Bound: A Doctor's Incredible Battle for Survival at the South Pole* (New York: Miramax, 2001).

Priestly, Rebecca, *Dispatches from Continent Seven: An Anthology of Antarctic Science* (Wellington, New Zealand: Awa Press, 2016).

Ronne, Edith M, *Antarctica's First Lady: Memoirs of the first American woman to set foot on the Antarctic continent and winter-over as a member of a pioneering expedition* (Beaumont, Texas: Clifton Steamboat Museum, 2004).

Ronne, Finn, *Antarctic Command* (New York: Bobbs-Merrill, 1961).

Ross, James Clark, *A voyage of discovery and research in the Southern and Antarctic regions, during the years 1839–43* (Cambridge, UK: Cambridge University Press, 2011).

Scott, Robert Falcon, *Journals: Captain Scott's Last Expedition*, Max Jones (ed) (Oxford, UK: Oxford University Press, 2008).

Shackleton, Ernest, *South: The Endurance Expedition* (New York: Signet Books, 1999).

Shackleton, Ernest, *The Heart of the Antarctic: The Farthest South Expedition, 1907–9* (New York: Signet Books, 2000).

Shirase Antarctic Expedition Supporters' Association, *The Japanese South Polar Expedition, 1910–12: A record of Antarctica* (Bluntisham: Bluntisham Books, 2011).

Siple, Paul, *90 Degree South: The Story of the American South Pole Conquest* (New York: Putnam, 1959).

Sullivan, Walter, *Assault on the Unknown: The International Geophysical Year* (New York: McGraw-Hill, 1961).

Swithinbank, Charles, *Vodka on Ice: A Year with the Russians in Antarctica* (London: Book Guild Publishing Ltd, 2002).

Walker, Gabrielle, *Antarctica: An Intimate Portrait of the World's Most Mysterious Continent* (London: Bloomsbury, 2012).

Weddell, James, *A Voyage towards the South Pole: Performed in the Years 1822–4: Containing an Examination of the Antarctic Sea, and a Visit to Tierra del Fuego* (New York: Cambridge University Press, 2011).

Wheeler, Sara, *Terra Incognita: Travels in Antarctica* (London: Vintage Publishing, 1997).

Wilkes, Charles et al, *United States exploring expedition, during the years 1838, 1839, 1840, 1841, 1842 under the command of Charles Wilkes* (Philadelphia: Lea and Blanchard C. Sherman, 1845).

BIOGRAPHIES AND SECONDARY ACCOUNTS

Caesar, Adrian, *The White: Last Days in the Antarctic Journeys of Scott and Mawson 1911–13* (Sydney: MacMillan, 1999).

Crane, David, *Scott of the Antarctic* (London: Harper Perennial, 2006).

Crawford, Janet, *That First Antarctic Winter: The Story of the Southern Cross Expedition of 1898–1900 as Told in the Diaries of Louis Charles Bernacchi* (Christchurch, New Zealand: South Latitude Research Limited, 1998).

Garde, François, *Paul-Émile Victor et la France de l'Antarctique* (Paris: Éditions Louis Audibert, 2006).

Huntford, Roland, *Scott and Amundsen* (New York: Putnam Publishing Group, 1981).

Lansing, Alfred, *Endurance: Shackleton's Incredible Voyage* (New York: Carroll & Graf Publishers, 1959).

Lowe, George and Lewis-Jones, Huw, *The Crossing of Antarctica: Original Photographs from the Epic Journey that Fulfilled Shackleton's Dream* (London: Thames & Hudson, 2014).

Maynard, Jeff, *Antarctica's Lost Aviator: The Epic Adventure to Explore the Last Frontier on Earth* (New York: Pegasus Books, 2019).

Roberts, David, *Alone on the ice: The greatest survival story in the history of exploration* (New York, New York: W. W. Norton & Company, 2014).

Rose, Lisle A, *Assault on Eternity: Richard E. Byrd and the Exploration of Antarctica, 1946–7* (Annapolis, Maryland: Naval Institute Press, 1980).

Sancton, Julian, *Madhouse at the End of the Earth: The Belgica's Journey into the Dark Antarctic Night* (New York: Crown, 2021).

Truswell, Elizabeth, *A Memory of Ice: The Antarctic Voyage of the Glomar Challenger* (Acton, Australia: ANU Press, 2019).

SCHOLARLY AND EDUCATIONAL WORKS

Anthony, Jason C, *Hoosh: Roast Penguin, Scurvy Day, and Other Stories of Antarctic Cuisine* (Lincoln: University of Nebraska Press, 2012).

Antonello, Alessandro, *The Greening of Antarctica: Assembling an International Environment* (Oxford: Oxford University Press, 2019).

Barczewski, Stephanie, *Antarctic Destinies: Scott, Shackleton, and the Changing Face of Heroism* (London: Continuum International Publishing Group, 2007).

Belanger, Dian Olson, *Deep Freeze: The United States, the International Geophysical Year, and the Origins of Antarctica's Age of Science* (Boulder: University Press of Colorado, 2006).

Brady, Anne-Marie, *China as a Polar Great Power* (Cambridge, UK: Cambridge University Press, 2017).

Burke, David, *Moments of Terror: The Story of Antarctic Aviation* (London: Robert Hale, 1994).

Clancy, Robert, Manning, John and Brolsma, Henk, *Mapping Antarctica: A Five Hundred Year Record of Discovery* (New York: Springer, 2014).

Day, David, *Antarctica: A Biography* (Oxford: Oxford University Press, 2012).

Dodds, Klaus, Hemmings, Alan D and Roberts, Peder (eds), *Handbook on the Politics of Antarctica* (Cheltenham: Edward Elgar Publishing, 2017).

Dodds, Klaus, *Pink Ice: Britain and the South Atlantic Empire* (London: I.B. Tauris, 2002).

Dowdeswell, Julian and Hambrey, Michael, *The Continent of Antarctica* (Winterbourne, Berkshire: Papadakis, 2018).

Fogg, GE, *A History of Antarctic Science* (Cambridge, UK: Cambridge University Press, 1992).

Fontana, Pablo, *La pugna antártica, el conflicto por el sexto continente: 1939–59* (Buenos Aires: Guazuvira Ediciones, 2014).

Foscari, Giulia, *Antarctic Resolution* (Zurich: Lars Müller Publishers, 2021).

Glasberg, Elena, *Antarctica as Cultural Critique: The Gendered Politics of Scientific Exploration and Climate Change* (New York: Palgrave Macmillan, 2012).

Griffiths, Tom, *Slicing the Silence: Voyaging to Antarctica* (Cambridge, MA: Harvard University Press, 2010).

Gurney, Alan, *Below the Convergence: Voyages Toward Antarctica 1699–1839* (New York: W. W. Norton & Company, 1997).

Headland, Robert K, *A Chronology of Antarctic Exploration: A Synopsis of Events and Activities from the Earliest Times until the International Polar Years, 2007–9* (London: Bernard Quaritch, 2009).

Howkins, Adrian, *Frozen Empires: An Environmental History of the Antarctic Peninsula* (Oxford: Oxford University Press, 2017).

Jones, AGE, *Antarctica Observed: Who Discovered the Antarctic Continent?* (Whitby, Yorkshire: Caedmon of Whitby, 1982).

Larson, Edward J, *An Empire of Ice: Scott, Shackleton, and the Heroic Age of Antarctic Science* (New Haven: Yale University Press, 2012).

Launius, Roger D, Fleming, James Rodger and DeVorkin, David H. (eds), *Globalizing Polar Science: Reconsidering the International Polar and Geophysical Years* (New York: Palgrave MacMillan, 2010).

Leane, Elizabeth, *South Pole: Nature and Culture* (London: Reaktion Books, 2016).

Lüdecke, Cornelia, *Germans in the Antarctic* (London: Springer Nature, 2021).

McCann, Joy, *Wild Sea: A History of the Southern Ocean* (Chicago: University of Chicago Press, 2019).

Pyne, Stephen J. *The Ice: A Journey to Antarctica* (Iowa City: University of Iowa Press, 1986).

Richards, Rhys, *Sealing in the Southern Oceans 1788–1833* (Wellington, NZ: Paremata Press, 2010).

Riffenburgh, Beau (ed), *Encyclopedia of the Antarctic, Vols 1&2* (New York: Routledge, 2007).

Roberts, Peder, van der Watt, Lize-Marié and Howkins, Adrian (eds), *Antarctica and the Humanities* (London: Palgrave Macmillan, 2016).

Roberts, Peder, *The European Antarctic: Science and Strategy in Scandinavia and the British Empire* (New York: Palgrave Macmillan, 2011).

Spufford, Francis, *I May Be Some Time: Ice and the English Imagination* (London: Faber and Faber, 1996).

Walton, David WH (ed), *Antarctic Science* (Cambridge, UK: Cambridge University Press, 1987).

FICTION

Alexander, Caroline, *Mrs. Chippy's Last Expedition: The Remarkable Journal of Shackleton's Polar-Bound Cat* (New York: Harper Perennial, 1999).

Arthur, Elizabeth, *Antarctic Navigation* (London: Bloomsbury, 2004).

Bainbridge, Beryl, *The Birthday Boys* (London: Penguin Books, 1991).

Batchelor, John C, *The Birth of the People's Republic of Antarctica* (New York: Henry Holt & Co., 1995).

Coleridge, Samuel Taylor and Doré, Gustave, *The Rime of the Ancient Mariner* (New York: Harper & Brothers, 1876).

Cooper, James Fenimore, *The Sea Lions: or, The Lost Sealers* (West Berlin, New Jersey: Townsend, 1860).

LeGuin, Ursula K, 'Sur' in *The Compass Rose* (Portland: Pendragon Press / Underwood Miller. 1982), pp.255–73.

Lovecraft, HP, *At the Mountains of Madness, and other novels* (Sauk City, WI: Arkham House, 1985).

McGregor, Jon, *Lean Fall Stand* (New York: Catapult, 2021).

Poe, Edgar Allan, *The Narrative of Arthur Gordon Pym of Nantucket* (New York: Penguin Classics, 1999).

Robinson, Kim Stanley, *Antarctica* (London: HarperCollins Publishers, 1998).

Semple, Maria, *Where'd You Go, Bernadette* (Boston: Little, Brown & Company, 2012).

Shelby, Ashley, *South Pole Station* (London: Picador, 2017).

Verne, Jules, *Le Sphinx des Glaces* (Paris: Hetzel, 1897).

ACKNOWLEDGEMENTS

In writing this book, we relied on the generous and gracious support of many people and institutions around the world.

First among these Nicholas Bell, Elysa Engelman, Paul O'Pecko and other staff of the Mystic Seaport Museum, Connecticut, involved in planning what should have been the flagship exhibition 'Discovering Antarctica, 1820–2020.' Cancelled due to the COVID pandemic, it is this project that allowed us to meet and to spend a year discussing how objects could be used to tell a global history of the Antarctic region, before this book had even been conceived.

Because no one is an expert in all aspects of Antarctic history or science, we depended heavily on the work of other writers and scholars. While our book does not include footnotes, nor a traditional bibliography, we hope that readers will seek out the work of these experts, some of whom we read and drew upon, some of whom pointed us in the direction of interesting objects or stories and some of whom read over our texts. They include Atholl Anderson, Alessandro Antonello, Michael Ashley, Matthew T Bamsey, Hester Blum, Marcus Brittain, Sankar Chatterjee, Marlene Cimons, Correne Coetzer, Lynne Cox, Paul Dayton, Klaus Dodds, Georges Gadioux, Huw Griffiths, Stephen Haddelsey, David Harrowfield, Robert Headland, Meredith Hooper, Adrian Howkins, Nomi Kaltmann, Elizabeth Leane, Bryan Lintott, Nelson Llanos, Cornelia Luedeke, Quiyarra McCahey, Hanne Nielsen, Olav Orheim, Eleanor Peers, Richard Phillips, Sarah Pickman, Stephen Pyne, Joanna Rae, Peder Roberts, Chet Ross, Morgan Seag, Erik Tammiksaar, Daphné Victor, Lize-Marié van der Watt and Bert Winther-Tamaki.

We are also indebted to the many people from around the world who have provided us with copies of their personal photographs. These images greatly enrich this work and were invaluable to our ability to represent the full diversity of Antarctic visitors. Thank you to Felicity Aston, Anne Bancroft, Julie Baum, Geoffrey Chen, Alfredo 'Alpio' Costa, Seb Coulthard, Duan Dewen, Justin Dodd, Rob Dunbar, Volkert Gazert, William Hammer, Tim Jarvis, the estate of Graham Knuckey, Kiya Riverman, David Rootes, Richard Phillips, Lewis Pugh, Matias Romero, the Ronne Family, Britney Schmidt, the Tribble Family, Adam Turner, Richard Turner, Paul Winberry and Andres Zarankin.

In addition, we benefited from the generosity of several artists who allowed us to reproduce their work in our book, including Lita Albuquerque, Jean de Pomereu, Sebastian Copeland, Lutz Fritsch, Anne Noble and Studio Orta.

As the authors of a book about history, we relied on images preserved by archives, museums and other institutions around the world. Although this list is not exhaustive, we would in particular like to thank the following people and their institutions: Christian Salewski, Alfred Wegener Institute; Ria Oliver, Antarctic Legacy of South Africa Archive; Bridget Rutherford, Antarctica New Zealand; Ieuan R Hopkins, Athena Dinar and Pete Bucktrout, British Antarctic Survey; Silvia Beatriz Acevedo, Correo Oficial de la República Argentina; Håkan Jorikson, Grenna Museum;

Joseph Cheek, International Polar Foundation; Aude Sonneville, Institut Polaire Français; Jiye Lim, Korea Polar Research Institute; Bruno Schelhaas, Leibniz Institute for Regional Geography; Julie Miller, Library of Congress; Sarah Applegate, Los Angeles Museum of Modern Art; Frédéric Perin, Météo France; Kendra Dean, Museum of Texas Tech University; Anders Bache, Roald Amundsens Hjem, Museene i Akershus; Lorena Aspé Bou, Museo Gabriel González Videla; Mary Anne Stets, Mystic Seaport; Brian Campbell, Eric Christian and Ian O'Neill, NASA; Cheryl D'Mello, National Centre for Polar and Ocean Research; Beatrice Okoro, National Maritime Museum; Richard Nunn, National Science Foundation Ice Core Facility; Francesca Eathorne, New Zealand Antarctic Heritage Trust; Gayle Strege, College of Education/Human Ecology Historic Costume and Textiles Collection, The Ohio State University; Camille Menaouer, Pacific Community; Genny LeMoine, Peary-MacMillan Arctic Museum; Tijun Zhang, Polar Research Institute of China; Claude de Broyer & Olivier Pauwels, Royal Belgian Institute of Natural Sciences; Joy Wheeler and Alasdair MacLeod, Royal Geographical Society; Ellen Embleton and Keith Moore, Royal Society; Naomi Boneham, Alex Partridge and Mia Surridge, Scott Polar Research Institute, University of Cambridge; Heidi Stover, Smithsonian Institution Archives; Erik Satrum, Smithsonian National Air and Space Museum; Joan Boudreau and Kay Peterson, Smithsonian National Museum of American History; David Dudfield, Wayne Marriott and the Iwi Liaison Komiti, Southland Museum and Art Gallery; Niho o te Taniwha; Lea French Davis and Pamela Overmann; United States Navy Heritage and History Command; Derek Quezada, University of California, Irvine Special Collections; Pablo de Leon, University of North Dakota; Giulia Foscari and Alberto Piovesan, UNLESS and D-Air Lab; Jim Madsen, Wisconsin IceCube Particle Astrophysics Center; Evan T Bloom, Woodrow Wilson International Center for Scholars.

We received an exceptional level support from everyone that we contacted, but a special debt of gratitude is owed to the following individuals for their patience and generosity: Elaine Hood, United States Antarctic Program; Kevin Roberts, British Antarctic Survey, Laura Kissel, Byrd Polar and Climate Research Center Archival Program, The Ohio State University; Charlotte Connelly and Lucy Martin, Scott Polar Research Institute, University of Cambridge, all of whom went above and beyond in their help and without whom this book could not have been finished.

Among the companies and non-governmental organisations who provided us with material or permissions to reproduce their brands, we thank: Burberry Limited; Chet Ross Rare Books; Engage Studios; Grayling; Greenpeace; Jonkers Rare Books; G. H. Mumm & Cie; Whyte & Mackay Limited.

We would also like to acknowledge our own research institutions, who supported us as we completed this work: Texas Tech University, where Daniella is Assistant Professor in Modern British History, and the Scott Polar Research Institute, University of Cambridge, where Jean is a Marie Skłodowska-Curie Research Fellow.

As we developed this book project, during a period of global uncertainty, Teasel Muir-Harmony, of the Smithsonian National Air and Space Museum, put us in touch with a number of publishers. Sarah Connelly, lately of Royal Museums Greenwich, connected us to Bloomsbury and we couldn't have been happier to work with a publisher so renowned for its maritime and historical books.

Thank you to Lee-May Lim and Richard Carr for their wonderful designs that bring to life each of our objects to their best advantage.

And of course, we would like to thank our editors at Bloomsbury, Kathryn Beer and Elizabeth Multon, whose enthusiasm and belief in our project gave us wings from day one. We could not have imagined a more generous involvement on their part, both in time and energy.

For those accidentally omitted from our acknowledgements, we apologise and still extend our thanks. We would also like to acknowledge our own limitations and failures in assembling this book.

Finally, we would like to thank our families. And Zoom.

INDEX